Walking in Love

A.B. SIMPSON

WALKING IN LOVE

*How to embrace
the very essence
of God*

Christian Publications
Camp Hill, Pennsylvania

Christian Publications
3825 Hartzdale Drive, Camp Hill, PA 17011

Faithful, biblical publishing since 1883

ISBN: 0-87509-578-X
LOC Catalog Card Number: 94-72911
© 1995 by Christian Publications
All rights reserved
Printed in the United States of America

95 96 97 98 99   5 4 3 2 1

Cover Photograph © 1995 by D. Jeanene Tiner

CONTENTS

The Preeminence of Love

And now these three remain: faith, hope and love. But the greatest of these is love. (1 Corinthians 13:13)

Our old English version has called love, charity. But the modern sense of that word has narrowed the glorious conception in the mind of the Holy Spirit when He wrote this sublime chapter. The heavenly charity means a great deal more than almsgiving, benevolence and sentimental love. The root of the word is the same as grace; it means that love which comes from heaven and is breathed into the heart by the Holy Spirit. It is not the love of human passion, but the grace of God and the nature of Christ. It is love as a gift and as an inwrought grace of the Holy Spirit. It is the queen of all the graces, to which even faith and hope must bow and before which they will fade away in the glory of eternal love. Why is love the greatest of these?

In Human Life and History

Love is the greatest thing in human life and history. What is the charm of poetry and romance? What has lit up the pages of literature in every age, and ever been the inspiration of the loftiest human genius? It has been the trials and the triumphs of human friendship and affection, the selfish sentiments often of unholy love. What is the meaning of patriotism? What has been the incentive that has carried millions of lives to the heroisms of the battlefield and made them count it a pride and joy to die for liberty and native land? It has been the love of country. What is the meaning of home, the dearest thing in human life? It is the embodiment of love; it is the place where all the holiest ties of life meet. Take away love from home, and it will pass out of existence, and life will become a dreary drudgery and a blank despair. So that literature, patriotism and home, perhaps the three greatest things in human life apart from God, are all expressions of love.

God has strangely placed in the hearts of men the ties and instincts of affection which bind them together in the social system. These instincts keep this great world moving in order and harmony, at the bidding of affections which men are called to obey, and without which human society would be a curse and a wreck. The world values love above all else. Many a man would give all he possesses for the love which he cannot buy; many a mother would be glad to be penniless to hold back from death the child that is more to her than life; many a woman is toiling and suffering amid hardships that no price could induce her to undergo, but counting it a luxury of joy for the man she loves and to whom she has given all her life. Oh, if the poor counterfeit, or, at least, the perverted and imperfect form which has been left to lost humanity as a wreck of love is so precious, what must the divine reality be?

In God

Love is the greatest thing in God. It is the only thing which is said in the Scriptures to be the nature or essence of God. God is righteous, holy, wise and mighty; but God is not holiness, wisdom and power (i.e., these attributes do not constitute His essence); but God is love. If you were to look at an embodiment of justice, it would not be God; it would only be one side of the mountain, precipitous and majestic, but terrible. But could you behold perfect love embodied, you would have God in all His fullness.

The predominant element in God is not righteousness, but love. Everything He has and does is dominated, controlled and colored by love. He is just, because He is love, and because injustice would be an injury and wrong to the creation. Where He can be just and also merciful, mercy rejoices against judgment.

As we look out upon the material universe, His goodness and kindness shine on every side and color every aspect of creation. And as we look at

His holy Word and the marvelous story of redemption, while it exhibits His holiness most marvelously, the picture of His love exceeds all else, and we are compelled to see what love is: "This is love: not that we loved God, but that he loved us and sent his Son as an atoning sacrifice for our sins" (1 John 4:10). And as we look at the story of each individual life and especially the lives of His children, we will find that God has been as kind as it was possible for Him to be in every case. He has done the very best possible for every human being, and even those, who at last perish through their unbelief, are the objects of His tenderest compassion. They perish against His will, and receive even in their ruin the tears of His tenderness and sorrow and the parting words of pathos, "How often I have longed to gather [you] together . . . but you were not willing" (Luke 13:34).

In the Holy Life and Character

Love is the greatest thing in the holy life and character. It is the sum of all duty and the summary of all law. "Love the Lord your God with all your heart and with all your soul and with all your mind and with all your strength" and "Love your neighbor as yourself" (Mark 12:30-31). This is the Lord's own exposition of His perfect law. And the greatest of the New Testament writers declares love is the fulfilling of law, for every commandment is briefly comprehended in this saying, namely, "Love your neighbor as yourself."

The Apostle John used to repeat the same sermon every Sabbath in the church, and it was one brief sentence only, "Little children, love one another." And when they asked him why he never said anything new, his answer was that there was nothing else to say, for this was the substance and summary of all Christ's commandments. Every grace is but a form of love—"The fruit of the Spirit is love, joy, peace, patience, kindness, goodness, faithfulness, gentleness and self-control" (Galatians 5:22-23)—but each of these is but a phase of love.

Joy is love exulting; peace is love reposing; patience is love enduring; goodness is the good manners of love; kindness is love in action; faithfulness is love confiding; gentleness is love yielding; and self-control is true self-love. If we would therefore have all the graces of the Spirit, we must have the root of all—the spirit of love—and all the branches will spring spontaneously from it and bear the heavenly fruits without effort or strain.

Incentive and Motive to Action

Love is the greatest incentive and motive to action, and is therefore the highest power in Christian life. How easy it is to get people to do things when you get their hearts! Sacrifice and labor are nothing to a loving heart, but without heart everything is drudgery. You cannot save a soul unless you love it. Your affection will become a bond to draw it to Christ. So God gives us the love of souls when He would enable us to win them. You cannot pray for another effectively without love; affection gives wings to devotion, and faith will be in proportion to love. You cannot endure the privations and toils of the Master's work in hard places without love. The service that Christ is asking from His people today is hard service, and only supreme love to God and intense devotion to Christ can carry you through the perils of the Sudan, the Congo or the climate of India.

Besides, love lifts us above a thousand distractions and hindrances in our work. Without it we will be constantly obstructed by annoyances, worries, injuries, wrongs and innumerable things which we will have to stop and regulate. But a loving heart moves on unhindered by any selfish consideration, seeking only to live for God and others, and leaving every other interest with Him. God cannot use people much without great love. It is the element of spiritual power immeasurably more than faith. The men and women who have been great soul winners and great missionaries have all been people of great hearts, specially anointed with the spirit of love.

The Element of Happiness

Love is the greatest element of happiness. The selfish heart is always unhappy. The true center of every life is not self, but something outside of self. God is the pattern of every other existence, and God's life is not for Himself, but the universe. Love is His principle and element, and He is ever giving. And so for every Christian life and every happy life the essential principle is, "It is more blessed to give than to receive" (Acts 20:35).

The fountains that are ever giving are ever full. Happy are they who have learned the secret of happiness, to live for God and others.

> Hast thou found some precious treasure?
>> Pass it on.
> Hast thou found some holy pleasure?
>> Pass it on.
> God Himself is ever giving,
> Loving is the truest living,
> Letting go is twice possessing,
> Would you double every blessing,
>> Pass it on.

The Loveliest Thing

Love is the loveliest thing in this world and the thing that speaks most for God in your life. Everybody can understand it. They may not know much about your deep experiences; they may not appreciate your shouts of joy and praise; but they can all feel the weight and value of your unselfish sacrifice and lovely acts. When you stand up in a crowded car to give your seat to some poor man or weary working woman, everybody understands it. Many a man will rise and raise his hat for some fashionably dressed young lady, but let the poor, weary washerwoman stand with her clothes basket for half an hour. But when you remember that everyone of these is perhaps a messenger whom Christ has sent to test you, you will find a thousand opportunities of speaking for Him that others miss. When you give up your lower berth in a Pullman car for some poor mother and child that might have to climb up to the top, you often find an opportunity of speaking to that mother of her soul that nothing else could give you. When you sit in the house of God with considerate thoughtfulness for the stranger and the poor whom you can, for a little sacrifice, make to feel more welcome, you do, perhaps, quite as much to lead them to Christ as the man who stands in the pulpit. When you show a loving, unselfish interest in your working man, your servant girl, the toiling man or woman that ministers to you in business relationships, there are a thousand little ways in which you can make them understand the spirit of your Christian life, and you can love them into the faith that they see working by love in you.

When Mr. Richards went to the Congo as a missionary, he spent six years trying to preach the natives into Christianity, but in vain. He went home to England to ask the advice of his friends how he could preach so as to save them. They told him to preach according to the theological books—to begin with the law and expound the Scriptures. He did so; he gave them a series of services on the Ten Commandments, and they said it was very good "chatter." They liked these commandments, but they still went on as before, living in dishonesty and sin.

Finally he gave up in despair, and went to God for light, and the Lord led him to begin with the gospel, which is the great commission of every missionary. He took the gospel of Matthew and began to expound it. He came to the verse, "Give to him that asketh thee, and from him that would borrow of thee turn not thou away" (Matthew 5:42, KJV). What was he to do? He could not expound it to them as it read unless he was willing to live it before them; but if he did he knew that they would take him at his word, as many of them were beggars and borrowers. He feared that within a few hours he would have nothing left in the house. But he was true to his commission. He preached the truth and told them that by the grace of God he meant to live it. They nodded assent and smiled approvingly; and after the service his wife came to him and insisted that if he was going to make a fool of himself, she, at least, would keep her things; so they were locked up in a room and the rest of the household goods were left open. Before sunset a crowd of natives came to see him. One by one, and before they all left, the house was empty. They had begged or borrowed or stolen everything he had, and had gone to their homes very much delighted with the white man and his religion.

But then God began to speak to their hearts, and they said one to another: "This is different from anything we ever heard. This must be God's man; and if this is God's man, we must be careful how we treat him"; and before long the goods were brought back again. He had acted on the principle of love and they felt they must do the same. The result was he had his goods back with interest and he had the hearts of all the people. Before long there was a revival in that place, and today there is a great church on the banks of the Congo that all grew out of that one man preaching and living the life of love. Surely the greatest of these is love.

The Chinese authorities and the American consul in China have borne testimony of the influence of another missionary in that land, who lived on the same principle and who was despised for it by most of his American friends as a crank and a fool. But after he had passed away, the highest authorities in the land bore witness that his life had done more to win them to the Christian religion than any other that had ever been known in that community.

> So let our lives and lips express
>   The holy gospel we profess;
> So let our works and actions shine
>   To show the doctrine all divine.

The Everlasting Attribute

Love is the everlasting attribute. Faith and hope will pass away, but love never.

> They sin who tell us love can die.
> With life all other passions fly,

But love is indestructible,
   Its holy flame ever burneth.
   From heaven it came, to heaven
     returneth.

Friend, what will you do in heaven without love? It will be too late to learn it there. God is teaching you now in the school of trial and provocation. Be sure you do not miss your lesson, for if you do not have it you can't get into heaven. God has determined to have one sweet place, and you may be sure He will have no cross, selfish people there. And so if you don't get out of your mean ways here, you will not find room in that world of love, and indeed without it you could not be happy there nor anywhere else. God help us to see our lack of love, to yield ourselves in entire surrender to His holy will in this highest and greatest of all His blessings, and then receive Jesus Himself as the living heart of our life and being, and then it shall be true of us:

   Live thou in love, so shall I give
   Thine own love back to thee.

The Love of God

This is love: not that we loved God, but that he loved us and sent his Son as an atoning sacrifice for our sins. (1 John 4:10)

But God demonstrates his own love for us in this: While we were still sinners, Christ died for us. (Romans 5:8)

But because of his great love for us, God, who is rich in mercy, made us alive with Christ even when we were dead in transgressions—it is by grace you have been saved. . . . in order that in the coming ages he might show the incomparable riches of his grace, expressed in his kindness to us in Christ Jesus. (Ephesians 2:4-5, 7)

We love because he first loved us. (1 John 4:19)

Our love must find its type and source in God. His love is the fountain of all other love and the unapproachable pattern. God's love is as indescribable as it is unapproachable. What language, what figure, what forms of speech or illustration can justly portray that which has neither measure nor limitation, which is an ocean without a shore, a depth without a fathoming line, an immensity without a border, a height, a depth, a length, a breadth which surpasses knowledge!

Someone has said in quaint and striking language:

> Could I with ink the ocean fill,
>   And were the sky of parchment made,
> Were every blade of grass a quill,
>   And every man a scribe by trade,
> To write the love of God above,
>   Would drain that ocean dry;
> Nor could the scroll contain the whole,
>   Though spread from sky to sky.

God has been writing His love on the sky and on the land. Every blade of grass is indeed a quill and every drop of the ocean an ink drop in which to write His love and every moment of our existence a blessed commentary upon it. But it will take eternity to unfold its boundless fullness and its infinite preciousness.

The Names and Terms

We see it in the very names and terms which are used to express it. God multiplies language in His effort to express and emphasize His great love. Just listen to a few of these expressions and see if there is anything like them in the Bible. No such language is used about His power, His wisdom, nor even His justice. They are again and again reiterated, but to express His love every possible form of speech is exhausted.

"The LORD, the LORD, the compassionate and gracious God, slow to anger, abounding in love and faithfulness, maintaining love to thousands, and forgiving wickedness, rebellion and sin" (Exodus 34:6-7). Again: "But because of his great love for us, God, who is rich in mercy, made us alive with Christ even when we were dead in transgressions" (Ephesians 2:4-5). And again: "That in the coming ages he might show the incomparable riches of his grace, expressed in his kindness to us in Christ Jesus" (2:7). Once more: "That you . . . may have power, together with all the saints, to grasp how wide and long and high and deep is the love of Christ, and to know this love that surpasses knowledge—that you may be filled to the measure of all the fullness of God" (3:17-19).

These are some of the various expressions used:

First, we have His mercy; that is love toward the unworthy and unlovely, the wicked and hateful and injurious, those that wrong Him, disobey

Him and cause Him only grief and pain. This is something that human love knows nothing of. We can love the amiable, the kind and lovely. "For a good man someone might possibly dare to die. But God demonstrates his own love for us in this: While we were still sinners, Christ died for us" (Romans 5:7-8). "But because of his great love for us, God, who is rich in mercy, made us alive with Christ even when we were dead in transgressions" (Ephesians 2:4-5). This is something that human reason cannot understand. It is the mystery of divine mercy that God should love the loveless and hateful, and that for those who are murdering Him He should pray, "Father, forgive them, for they do not know what they are doing" (Luke 23:34). This is the miracle of Christian love, that it can obey the precept, "Love your enemies, do good to those who hate you, bless those who curse you, pray for those who mistreat you" (6:27-28). But only those who have received His Spirit into theirs and learned His nature can do it.

Grace is used to express His love. Grace means the love that expects no return, that is given to those who are helpless and could do nothing either to deserve it or compensate it. We read of the riches of His grace, "the incomparable riches of his grace" (Ephesians 2:7).

The word *goodness* describes the activities of love, the positive and actual expressions of it in kind and helpful acts and words. Goodness is love in action, and how good God is! How much He has done for our happiness and well-being!

The word *kindness* is used. This means kinship. It refers to the attitude in which He places us. He treats us as His relatives, as His children, as members of His household and partners of His very life, taking us into His innermost intimacy, and loving us as children, as the very bride of His affection.

But the best of all these words is love. It expresses His delight in those He loves. Love is the outgoing of the whole heart with intense joy and delight in those on whom it bestows its affections. And God really loves us, takes delight in us, treats us as He would treat His own beloved Son and makes us partakers of all that He has. "For the LORD's portion is his people" (Deuteronomy 32:9). He finds His satisfaction and His joy in their love and blessing.

And when all terms have been exhausted, and all adjectives and adverbs have been piled like mountain on mountain in the great climaxes which vainly seek to express His great heart, He sums it all up in the inexpressible words, "this love [of Christ] that surpasses knowledge" (Ephesians 3:19).

From His Works

We learn His love from His works. All nature is a revelation of the divine goodness. It is true that sin has introduced many a dark shadow, many a seeming contradiction to the divine goodness; but notwithstanding all, even the story of creation and the volume of nature unite on every page in proclaiming the God of love. Everywhere we see the traces of a decline and fall from a state of perfection. Nature itself reveals the fact that the present condition of things was not primeval, and there must once have been some better age from which the universe has fallen. But even amid the wreck, how much there is that speaks of His goodness! How much of beauty we behold in the heavens and earth! How much of happiness! Even the blossoming flower and the singing bird cannot keep back their tributes to the Creator who has made them to be beautiful and happy.

Look at your own physical organism and think of its numerous senses and organs. He might easily have made every sense of your body to be a channel of anguish, as they become when distorted by disease. But instead He has made them to be the vessels and channels of pleasure. He might have made the food you eat merely to nourish you without gratifying you, but He has created you so that it ministers the keenest pleasure to your taste. He might have made everything taste alike, but instead of this He has created innumerable varieties of fruits and food for your gratification. He has filled the air with sweet odors that satisfy the sense of smell. He has adopted the blue of heaven and the green of earth to soothe and satisfy your eye. He has adjusted your ear for all the delicate varieties of sound, and He has fitted the external world to minister to this sense with a thousand melodious notes. He has given you affections and He has met them by the ties of home and the friendships of life. He has placed within you instincts and faculties of disposition and of mind, and He has fitly framed you into a world of social life where you find room for the development and exercise of these faculties and powers.

Everywhere His natural laws are obeyed we find harmony and happiness and the evidences of His loving plan to minister to our happiness and to promote our highest well-being. The very men and women who are disobeying Him and blaspheming Him and doing all in their power to grieve and dishonor Him owe to Him every thrill of joy that stirs their being, every physical enjoyment even in their sinful pleasures, every delight that comes to them in the friendships and affections which they prostitute to His dishonor, and which He yet allows to minister as far as He can to their gratification.

From His Ways and Providences

We learn the love of God from His ways and providences as much as from His works. His government of this universe is as gracious as was His creating goodness. How kindly He has held these mighty worlds from collision and destruction! How perfect the order and harmony of nature in its great physical laws! How beneficent these laws when obeyed, and how adapted even their penalties are to keep us from harming ourselves! Even the things that hurt us are kind, because they are meant to keep us back from danger. God has made the very fire to burn us so that we may be warned from destruction, and He has surrounded our path with a thousand little thorns simply to save us from stepping into greater dangers. How wonderful His government of this world!

Even the story of heathen nations is full of beautiful touches of the divine providence. How wisely and graciously God has planned the great movements of nations and armies to bring about His great purpose of love for the world. The story of Egypt and Assyria, of Babylon and Persia, of Greece and Rome, all show a hand ever moving for the special purpose of goodness and mercy toward those who trusted God. How wonderful His care of Moses and Israel! How marvelous the story of Esther and her people in the days of the Persian Empire! How thrilling the story of Christian history through the centuries, with its countless illustrations of the divine interpolation in love and grace to protect and deliver His trusting people! How full of God's love the story of your life and the providences through which He has led you, and how truly each of us can say:

Ten thousand thousand precious gifts
  My daily thanks employ,
Nor is the least a cheerful heart
  That tests these gifts with joy.
Through all eternity to Thee,

A joyful song I'll raise,
But oh! eternity's too short
To utter all Thy praise!

From His Words

We learn the love of God from His words. It is
thus we learn the love of our friends, their kind
expressions to us, their assurances of regard, their
promises, their encouragements, their tender
messages of affection by letter or voice. How we
cherish these words, and how much of joy and
happiness can radiate from a single line or a
single tone of one who loves us! And so God
knows how to speak His love. His precious Word
is full of gracious messages which every believing
heart can receive as His personal assurances of
love. The Bible is God's love letter to the heart of
faith, and we read its promises as directed to ourselves. And God does not rebuke our holy
freedom, but loves to have us take Him at His
word and put our names in every promise.

What wonderful words He has spoken! There
is nothing in human literature that sounds like
the promises of the Bible. There is a sweet
cadence in them and a holy tenderness that
separates them from all human speech. Read the
writings of Plato, the fragments of Socrates, the
sayings of Confucius or Buddha, the philosophy
of Seneca, and you will find no such sentences as
these: "The LORD appeared to us in the past
saying, 'I have loved you with an everlasting love;
I have drawn you with loving-kindness' "

(Jeremiah 31:3). There is something in that sentence which carries its own divinity with it and speaks with a self-manifesting light as the very voice of God.

Or again, "Come to me, all you who are weary and burdened, and I will give you rest" (Matthew 11:28). There is nothing ever uttered by mortal lips that speaks like that. We feel as we listen to it that it must come from a greater heart than mortal. He who utters it must be divine and His name must be Love.

Or once more, listen to Him as He speaks again: "Do not let your hearts be troubled. Trust in God; trust also in me. In my Father's house are many rooms; if it were not so, I would have told you. I am going there to prepare a place for you" (John 14:1-2). "I will not leave you comfortless: I will come to you" (14:18, KJV). Surely there is a dignity and yet a tenderness in words like these that carry the heart of God with them and speak His tender love as no other words can speak it.

Then there are His gracious promises. How wonderfully they are adapted to prove His love! How He has fenced in the poor sinner with words that almost compel him to take salvation! How often we have thought, when sitting down by some poor trembling soul, of the wonderful words of love that enable us to lead him to Christ and that render it almost impossible for him to escape the resistless logic of divine mercy!

Take, for example, such promises as this: "Whoever comes to me I will never drive away"

(6:37). The doubting heart cannot get away from it. There is no possible excuse or pretext for doubting, no matter how unworthy, no matter how weak the trust, no matter how long he has been in coming. It is simple and explicit: "Whoever comes to me I will never drive away."

Or take again that precious promise: "If we confess our sins, he is faithful and just and will forgive us our sins and purify us from all unrighteousness" (1 John 1:9). It does not matter what the sin is; all we have to do is confess it. It does not say, if we feel very sorrowful, if we have very strong faith, if we have good resolutions, if we never repeat the sin again, but simply, "If we confess our sins." The soul is shut up by divine love to receive forgiveness and is compelled to lay its burden down and go away rejoicing and believing. The ingenuity of mercy could not go farther in contriving to compel poor sinful hearts to be saved and to be happy.

So again, His promises for the sorrowing, the tried, the tempted, are so various and countless that there is no possible situation for which His love has not provided some word in season. Are you tempted? "He will not let you be tempted beyond what you can bear. But when you are tempted, he will also provide a way out" (1 Corinthians 10:13). Are you anxious? You are bidden to take no anxious thought, but to "Cast all your anxiety on him because he cares for you" (1 Peter 5:7). Are you insufficient for your burdens and pressures? He declares, "My grace is sufficient for you, for my power is made perfect in weakness" (2 Corinthians 12:9). Are you desolate and forsaken? He meets us with the promise, "Never will I leave you; never will I forsake you" (Hebrews 13:5). Are you conscious of unworthiness? He tells us, "I want you to know that I am not doing this for your sake, declares the Sovereign LORD. Be ashamed and disgraced for your conduct, O house of Israel!" (Ezekiel 36:32).

Have you wandered from the way? He tells us, "He is able to deal gently with those who are ignorant and are going astray" (Hebrews 5:2), and that He is our Shepherd, restoring our soul and making us to walk in the right paths for His own name's sake. Are you afraid? He says to us again and again, "So do not fear, for I am with you; do not be dismayed, for I am your God" (Isaiah 41:10). "Whoever listens to me will live in safety and be at ease, without fear of harm" (Proverbs 1:33). Have you a thousand needs for which your resources are inadequate? He says, "My God will meet all your needs according to his glorious riches in Christ Jesus" (Philippians 4:19).

And so His words of love are infinite and full. And in proportion to our trials and difficulties do we find their preciousness and all-sufficiency; so that we can say with the beloved in the Song of Songs: "His mouth is sweetness itself; he is altogether lovely" (5:16); or with the Psalmist, "How precious to me are your thoughts, O God! How vast is the sum of them! Were I to count them, they would outnumber the grains of sand" (139:17-18).

Then how often the blessed Spirit brings to us His words in more tender and personal messages, whispered to our heart, breathing the comfort, the instruction, the correction, the love we need, and making the written Word a living message from the mouth of the Living God. If God had done nothing else to show His love than to give us the Bible, He would have bound our hearts to Him by as many ties as the tens of thousands of promises which it contains.

The Highest Manifestation of Love

But God's highest manifestation of His love is in redemption. Christ and Calvary are the crowning commendation of the divine love. "God demonstrates his own love for us" (Romans 5:8), not by talking about it so much as by this highest pledge, the gift of infinite and everlasting love. "God so loved the world that he gave his one and only Son, that whoever believes in him shall not perish but have eternal life" (John 3:16). That little word "so" is an ocean without a shore, an immensity without a boundary. It is something that cannot be explained nor emphasized by human words. It speaks for itself and bids us bow in silent wonder, and say:

> Love so amazing, so divine,
> Demands my soul, my life, my all.

That cross stands like some great unapproachable mount that, as we look at it from every side, grows ever more wonderful and yet more impossible to paint or picture.

Shall we think of its infinite and amazing cost? Shall we think of the majesty and glory of that gift? God's only Son, and then of the suffering and shame to which He was given—the cruel cross, the awful grave, the curse of sin and its vengeance due to the whole guilty race? Shall we think of the long years during which He was separated from heaven, as well as the hours of agony through which He hung upon Calvary? Shall we think of the stupendous descent He made when He left the throne of Deity and became forever part of the human race—the Creator, one of a race of sinful, degraded creatures, whose very name in the heavens must have been linked with shame and disgrace?

Shall we think of the gladness with which He came and made that mighty sacrifice? Shall we remember the eternal love in that Father's heart which planned and purposed it all, and then sent Him to accomplish it? Redemption was not an afterthought with God, nor did He need to be constrained to give His consent to the salvation of our race because some satisfaction had been given that appeased His vengeance. But the wonderful plan for human redemption was His own design. The coming of Jesus was His eternal thought. This wonderful redemption was the project of His own everlasting love. Think of the value of the blessings it has brought us! In that gift all other gifts are pledged, for "He who did not spare his own Son, but gave him up for us all—how will he not also, along with him, graciously give us all things?" (Romans 8:32).

And finally, shall we put our own name into all this and remember that the love which caused Jesus to die was not a general love for humanity as a whole, but it was a personal love for each of us? That sacrifice was for you and for me. He who hung on that cross was thinking of you and of me when He wept and died. This great love is all for us as individuals, and each can say, "He loved me and gave Himself for me."

In Our Salvation and Daily Life

God shows us His love by His grace in our salvation and our daily Christian life. How wonderful His love in our salvation! Little would it have availed us for Christ to die on Calvary had the Holy Spirit not come and sought and found us in our sin and brought us to the Savior. How long He had to seek some of us! Half a century we had resisted Him until He had to follow us through all the changes and degradations of a ruined life. Step by step we sank deeper and deeper in our guilt and misery and wandered farther and farther from His pleadings till, at last, we sank so low that there was nothing left but to go to Him. Then we found Him ready and waiting, unwearied with all our wicked rejection, and more than willing to take charge of our life and give us back the fullness of His grace and the glories of His heaven. How we love Him for saving us! How we bless the hand that sometimes had to hurt us in order to turn us back from ruin! How gently and tenderly He welcomed us! How sweet the memory of forgiveness and the new joy of His first appearing to our broken hearts! And then, how great the love that took us up and led us on until this day.

Were I to lay an orphaned child at your door this morning and expect you to take it and keep it all its days, to be responsible for its food and clothing, its education and future prospects, you would think I was asking a good deal. And if I were to bring one every day, you would soon ask to be excused from such a strain upon your generosity. But every soul that comes to Christ is infinitely more trouble to Him than any child to mother or foster mother. He has to take you for better or for worse and carry you all the coming years. And how much trouble He has had with some of us! He takes you knowing all that is to come, all your failures, dispositions, temptations, backslidings, all the times you will doubt Him, disobey Him, wander from Him, grieve Him, go into perils that will almost ruin your soul and cause Him infinite trouble in bringing you back.

And yet, knowing all, He takes you forever and will never let you go. Oh! the tender grace He has shown to some of us! Oh! the memories that crowd upon us of His faithful love, so that we can say like David, "I will remember you from the land of Jordan, the heights of Hermon—from Mount Mizar" (Psalm 42:6). How many times He has taken us up into the mountain heights of Hermon and shown us the vision of His glory!

And how many times He has met us at some little hill and given us some blessing that was more touching even than the greater manifestations of His love and power! How He has shown us His love in restoring us from temptations and wanderings! How often has His love shone forth in the hour of sorrow, when He has come to us as "the God of all comfort" (2 Corinthians 1:3), and, "as a mother comforts her child" (Isaiah 66:13), wiping away our tears and healing our broken hearts!

And how often when there was no sorrow He has made us glad by His communion and His presence. As a mother would pick up her little child and love it and press it to her bosom just because it was so dear, so He has often come to us and filled us with such a strange, sweet joy that we could not understand, and then He has made us to know it is just because He loved us and delighted in us and wanted us to know how dear we were to Him! How good and kind He has been in answering our prayers! Our life is filled with the records and memories of His faithfulness. How many memorials lie along our path, like Ebenezer's, each one crying:

Come, Thou Fount of every blessing,
Tune my heart to sing Thy grace;

Streams of mercy never ceasing,
Call for songs of loudest praise.

The Glory That Awaits Us

God's love is yet to be more gloriously displayed in the glory that awaits us, for He has begun with us an everlasting story. His love will never, never, never end. His heart has planned for us blessing upon blessing through ages upon ages forever. Just beyond us lies the bright millennial age, 1,000 years of sinless, deathless joy and blessedness. But this is only the beginning of eternal ages. Beyond that bright millennial sunset lies a brighter morning, and, beyond that, eon after eon of mightier, holier, grander felicities and glories, not only on this green earth, but perhaps in the dominion of the stars and constellations which, perhaps, in the new heavens, is to be our eternal home.

Yes, He has saved us, that "in the coming ages he might show the incomparable riches of his grace, expressed in his kindness to us in Christ Jesus" (Ephesians 2:7). Were we to behold the vision of that glory now it would be more than we could bear! Someday we will understand it, and amid its wonders and splendors we will begin to know the boundless and everlasting love of God.

And now, in conclusion, what does all this mean for us? First, it means that God expects us to believe in His love and never to doubt nor question Him. In human friendship it is very delightful to be able to feel that we never doubted our friend or that we never were doubted by our friends. We all have some dear one whom we have never doubted, and it would seem to us an awful crime even to imagine a doubt against him. We have some friends who have never doubted us. We value the love and confidence of those who, under the severest strain, have never questioned us. If someone who has known me for a lifetime came to me and said, "I have confidence in you because I have investigated your character and believe from evidence that it is good," I would scarcely value his regard. But if he came to me in the dark days of calumny and cruel slander, and said, "My brother, I know you. I trust you, and I cannot distrust you," I would feel that he was indeed a friend. Thank God for a few such friends. Thank God for some hearts that have never even been tempted to doubt, because back of their trust was a love they could not question.

That is what God expects of us. Sometimes our trust is tried by the strangest outward appearances, but that is just the time He wants us to trust Him most; for often behind these seeming contradictions and painful providences lies the deepest purpose of blessing. Therefore:

> If He sometimes sends us chastening,
>   If He sometimes must reprove,
> It is just because He loves us
>   With an everlasting love.

Second, He wants us to live in the element and atmosphere of His love. He wants us to have a communion with Him so close that we never remember a frown. I remember, when a school boy, how I prided myself on never being punished by my teacher. There was a delicate confidence between us which I could not bear to have broken. Had he been compelled to chastise me, I would have felt that something was lost that never could be regained. Never again could I have looked into his face with quite the same delight. And so, God wants us to be the same with Him, the children of unbroken confidence, so close to Him, so uninterrupted in our obedience and confidence that the precious promise will indeed be true for us, "I have sworn not to be angry with you, never to rebuke you again" (Isaiah 54:9). Jesus has said to us, "As the Father has loved me, so have I loved you. Now remain in my love" (John 15:9).

Two things will keep this evermore. One, simple trust, and the other, implicit obedience. Let us never doubt His love, and let us never disobey His will. So will we ever dwell in love and in God, and it will be true of us for evermore:

> Living in the love, the love of Jesus,
>   Leaning upon His breast,
> Walking in His holy will each moment,
>   This is a heaven of rest.

The Love of the Divine Trinity

*He who loves me will be loved by my Father,
and I too will love him and show myself to
him. (John 14:21)*

*I write to you, fathers, because you have
known him who is from the beginning. . . . I
write to you, dear children, because you have
known the Father. (1 John 2:13)*

The love of the Spirit. (Romans 15:30)

These three verses speak distinctively of the love of the Father, of the Son and of the Spirit and of our personal knowledge of the three persons of the Godhead.

There is something very wonderful in personality. What is the difference between you and your neighbor? You may be just alike in features, form and stature, but one of you is inexpressibly dear to me, the other a matter of indifference. You have 10 children, but each one is a distinct world of interest and love to you. You do not love them all together, but you love each one with your whole heart. If one is taken from you another cannot supply its place. You know the voice, the touch, the step of your friend and the very name and memory wake up a thousand throbbing thoughts and feelings. There is one woman in the world who fills all your heart and is interlinked with all your life. There are thousands of others more beautiful, more cultivated, more gifted than she, but none can take her place. Her personality is her own and you know her from all others, and even her touch is different to you. And so God has created a universe of persons, each a little world, unique, alone, a strangely solemn immortal "I," so dependent, yet so independent, so associated, yet so isolated, so bound up with other hearts and yet in some respects so strangely, utterly alone.

This strange fact of personality has its beginning in God Himself. God is a person, not a principle, not an embodiment of virtues and attributes, but a living being, an actual subsistence, a heart as sensitive and real as your own. God is not only one person, but three. In the divine family, if we might dare to use such a term, there is a Father, there is a Mother, and there is a Son, and that Son is a Brother and a Bridegroom, so that every human relationship in a measure is represented in a glorious and sacred Trinity. How three can be one is not so great a mystery even in human experience. On that bench three men can sit together and constitute one court, and if their judgments were always identical and their thoughts always parallel the unity would be perfect. And so, on that eternal throne there sits a Godhead consisting of three persons, each an individual, and yet together a unity, never differing in thought, purpose, nor feeling, the glorious Three in One.

In a family there may be three persons: the father, mother and son. If they should always agree in purpose, plan and conception and affection, they too would be a copy in miniature and in perfection of the Godhead. Each of them has his or her distinctive personality and yet all are one.

So in the Divine Trinity, the Father has offices and attitudes which the Son cannot exercise nor sustain, and the Holy Spirit has relationships which the Father cannot fill, and the blessed Son has a place which neither the Father nor the Spirit can touch. And yet they are ever one although ever distinct. Each is a living individual existence, possessing all the power and all the perfection of the other, and yet all ever cooperating in perfect accord and inseparable unity.

Now, each of these divine persons is personally related to us with a distinctive bond of intimacy and fellowship. We read in these verses of the love of the Father, the love of the Son and the love of the Spirit. We read here of knowing "him who is from the beginning" (1 John 2:13), that is the Son, and also of the "dear children [who] have known the Father" (2:13).

Some of us can remember a time in our experience when we tried to grasp the doctrine of the Trinity, and our intellect sank oppressed under its tremendous weight. We went to God in helplessness and almost in despair, and then there came to us something so different, and yet so satisfactory. It was a personal revelation of God in His threefold personality.

The blessed Son was revealed to us, and we knew Jesus not only in His humanity, but in His deity as our individual Friend, whose person we could recognize distinctly from all others, and whose love thrilled our heart with a joy above all other.

Then the Father was revealed to us through the Son, and yet distinct from the Son, a glory inaccessible and infinite from whose bosom came that other glory, the incarnate Christ. We knew the Father and the Son who dwelt in the bosom of the Father.

And then there came to us a third revelation more insensible, if possible, than the others, but most distinct and conscious. We knew that there was a person that had made Jesus real to us, that had shed abroad the love of the Father in our heart; there was a hand that was unfolding the vision; there was a light that was illuminating the picture; there was a person that was bringing us into the presence of the Father and the Son, and that was the blessed Holy Spirit. That Spirit Presence so peaceful, so modest, so self-hiding,

so gentle, so considerate of our own personal in-
dependence as not to do violence to any of our
faculties, came in sweet accord with our whole
being and approached us through our own
spiritual sensibilities. It was the blessed Holy
Spirit, and we have come to know that Spirit as
our innermost consciousness and our dearest and
nearest Friend.

And now we understand the Trinity, not
through abstract conception, not through intellectual perception, not as a dogma that we could
write or talk about, but as a blessed, satisfying fellowship. We know our Father, we know our
Mother, we know our Brother and Bridegroom,
and we have come into the fellowship of the
mystery of God the Father and of Christ.

As we venture for a little to touch these
separate cords, to unfold in the language of the
Scripture itself these various aspects of the divine
being and the divine love, may the Holy Spirit
Himself awaken in each of us a responsive touch,
and may this become the interpreter to us of
words which otherwise would be too high and
deep for us to comprehend!

The Father's Love

1. Chosen in Him

Away back in the most distant ages that love
began, we were chosen in Him before the foundation of the world. Our love is not a second
thought nor the result of Christ's redeeming

work, but the primary cause of it and the original thought of our everlasting Father. Before the mountains were built, before the earth was made, He loved us and purposed our creation, redemption and glory. He has never had any other thought for us than the one first and highest purpose of everlasting love. Each of us can look back and remember that it was true of us, "The LORD appeared to us in the past, saying: 'I have loved you with an everlasting love' " (Jeremiah 31:3).

2. *Accepting Us in Christ*

His love is shown next by His accepting us in Christ, forgiving our sins and justifying us freely by His grace. This love is unfolded to us in the Savior's picture of the prodigal's return and the father's welcome. This is the Father's reclaiming love, a love so tender that He blots out the very consciousness of our sin and takes us at once to the nearest and highest place, refusing to listen to our wretched complaints and conditions or to permit us to take the place of a servant, opening to us all the fullness of a Father's heart and a Father's house. "He hath made us accepted in the beloved" (Ephesians 1:6, KJV). This is very strong language; literally it is "in the Son of His love." Therefore, we are accepted even as the Son of His love and are as dear as He.

3. *Recognizing Us as Sons*

The Father manifests His love in begetting us and recognizing us as His sons. This is a marvelous love over which even the Apostle John, who lived in the bosom of his Father, stands amazed, exclaiming, "How great is the love the Father has lavished on us, that we should be called children of God!" (1 John 3:1). And then he adds, "Now are we children of God" (3:2). We are not only called, but we are the sons of God. This is a rank that angels cannot claim; this is a place that Adam never knew. This is to be partaker of the divine nature and even of God Himself. As His sons we are entitled to His peculiar love, almighty protection, bountiful provision and everlasting faithfulness. Your child is not related to you by a contingent bond. He cannot cease to be your child. He may dishonor you, he may disobey you, he may need to be disciplined by you, but he is forever your child and loved the most when most unworthy.

Oh, how strange and tender, how strong and sweet this everlasting love of the Father!

4. Training, Educating and Disciplining Us

The Father shows His love to us by training us, educating us, disciplining us. And so we read in the epistle to the Hebrews of son-training. It is called "chastening" in our verses, but this is an unfortunate translation. The Greek calls it *paideia*, which means "the training of a child." And so God educates us as His sons. Sometimes the lessons are hard, sometimes the hours are long, sometimes the tasks are imperative, and sometimes the rod may even be applied, but it is all in the Father's love. There is a great difference between the discipline of the prison and the discipline of the school. One is penal and the other is parental. Our Father's chastenings are always in love.

The Queen of England sent her son to learn to be a mariner. He had to stand before the mast and to do hard service on the stormy deck, but it was for his good. Those hardships were to make him manly and fit him for his future station. You send your boy to school when it would be more pleasant for him to play in the yard. But you require him to undergo severe discipline and fulfill laborious tasks because you love him. You are training your boy for manly service in the great field of life, and you do not count it a hardship, but a great opportunity. And so your Father's discipline is loving, faithful, indispensable and thorough. "No discipline seems pleasant at the time, but painful. Later on, however, it produces a harvest of righteousness and peace for those who have been trained by it" (Hebrews 12:11).

5. *Shown to Those Who Obey*

The Father shows His peculiar love to those that obey Him and receive the Lord Jesus in His fullness. There is a wonderful promise in this passage in John, "If anyone loves me, . . . my Father will love him" (14:23). God's love to us is graduated according to our obedience and fidelity to Jesus. God's mercy in saving us is without respect of persons, but after we become His children He recompenses us by His greatest reward, His own love and approval, according to our obedience. Therefore, Jesus Himself said, "[The Father] has not left me alone, for I always do what pleases him" (8:29). Christ's obedience won for Him the delight of His Father, and He still delights in every loving and obedient child. If you would constantly enjoy His approving smile, let Him see a spirit of single-hearted devotion to Jesus and uncompromising and unqualified obedience to His will.

6. *Intimately United to His Son*

The Father's highest love is manifested to those who are most intimately united to the person of His Son.

Our union with Jesus and His constantly abiding in us will bring to us the same love which the Father has for Him. Therefore we read these wonderful words in the parting prayer of the Son of man, "I [am] in them and you in me. . . . to let the world know that you . . . have loved them even as you have loved me" (17:23). The same love which the Father has for Jesus He has for those in whom Jesus fully dwells. It is not you He loves. There is nothing in you to love. But it is the image, no, the very presence of His Son in you that He delights in. Just as that father loves his child, in a measure, because it is part of the mother's life and that mother is the dearest object of his affection, so God loves you because He sees in you the face of Jesus, the Spirit of Jesus and the life of Jesus. It is, therefore, Christ love and Christ life.

If we have received Christ to abide within us, we may know that we are as dear to our Father as He is. We can go to Him in holy confidence and boldness and know the meaning of those wondrous words, "So that we will have confidence on the day of judgment, because in this world we are like him" (1 John 4:17). The very place of Jesus in His bosom is ours. Like Him we may think of ourselves as lying "at the Father's side" (John 1:18), and we, too, may be "filled with delight day after day, rejoicing always in his presence" (Proverbs 8:30).

Oh, what a place we may have in the Father's love! Shall we claim it and in it shall we find our portion and our joy?

The Love of Jesus

1. *Self-sacrificing Love*

It is a self-sacrificing love: "He loved me and gave himself for me." This is a wonderful truth when the Holy Spirit makes it personal to us and we see and feel that it was for each of us that He thus died, that His love was personal, that He actually thought of us when He hung upon that cruel tree.

2. *A Seeking and Saving Love*

His love is a seeking and saving love. He loves us before we come to Him, and His love follows us until it finds us. How patient, how ingenuous, how untiring the love of Jesus for the sinner! See Him as He seeks and finds the hardhearted Zacchaeus and breaks him all to pieces with His love. See Him as He conquers the proud heart of Saul and binds him eternally to His own heart by bonds of grateful love. Think of His love to the mighty host of sinful men and women who have been subdued by it and transformed into saints and servants. Think how He loved us and sought and found us. It is the love of the Good Shepherd missing the lost one and going after it until He finds it.

3. A Keeping Love

It is a keeping love. What infinite trouble He has with us! How much thought and care we cause Him! How much He has to bear with us and from us! How often we disappoint Him! How often we risk our very souls by disobedient presumption and heedlessness! How rich the grace which He bestows upon us! How unceasing the intercession He is exercising for us at God's right hand! How infinite the blessing that He pours upon our heads! It is probably true that no single blessing ever reaches us without coming through His name and receiving the endorsement of His hand upon the check before it passes Heaven.

4. A Sympathetic Love

It is a sympathetic love. It is a love that has

entered into our very nature and life. It has made Him partaker of our humanity and brought Him down to Bethlehem and Calvary. "We do not have a high priest who is unable to sympathize with our weaknesses, but we have one who has been tempted in every way, just as we are" (Hebrews 4:15). "He is able to deal gently with those who are ignorant and are going astray, since he himself is subject to weakness" (5:2). He who wept at Lazarus' tomb still shares our every sorrow.

> He who wept and prayed in anguish,
>   In Gethsemane,
> Drinks with us each cup of trembling,
>   in our agony.
> Yesterday, today, forever,
>   Jesus is the same;
> All may change, but Jesus never!
>   Glory to His name!

5. A Love for Those Who Are His

Jesus has a special love for those who are entirely His own. For He as well as the Father declares in John 14 He gives His love as a reward to the obedient heart and to the one that gives Him right of way. He says, "If anyone loves me, he will obey my teaching. My Father will love him, and we will come to him" (14:23). He says again, "You are my friends if you do what I command" (15:14). There is an inner circle of the absolutely obedient ones and the hearts that are always true;

to these the Master gives His peculiar love. It is when Christ dwells in your heart and you have your being rooted and grounded in love that you are able to "grasp how wide and long and high and deep is the love of Christ, and to know this love that surpasses knowledge" (Ephesians 3:18-19).

6. A Love of Intimacy

It is a love of peculiar intimacy. He calls Himself by many tender names—three especially, our Friend, our Brother and our Bridegroom. All that these tender names mean of holy human affection, Jesus is to us. The highest of all is the Bridegroom's love. He calls us His sister, His spouse, or rather His sister spouse. There is something deeply sacred, sweet and holy in this combination. It is the union of the passionless love of the brother with the ardent affection of the husband. All that is earthly is taken out of it, all that is loving and tender is added to it.

Do we know Him in this way? Can we say of Him in all these endearing aspects, "This is my beloved and this is my friend"?

The Love of the Spirit

1. The Picture of a Mother

If Jesus is the Brother and Bridegroom, the Holy Spirit is represented in the Bible under the picture of a mother. The allusion in the third chapter of John to our being born of the Spirit is most distinct in this direction, and the very picture is full of tenderness. All we know of the Holy Spirit is in the direction of gentleness and love. The favorite emblem, the dove, is suggestive of nothing but tenderness. For the love of the Spirit needs no other proof than the very fact that for centuries this blessed One has chosen for His abode this uncongenial world of sin and sorrow. Scarcely do we realize, perhaps, that while the Second Person of the Trinity condescended to live on earth for 33 years, the Third Person has had no other home since the time of Christ.

2. *Calling the Sinner*

But no less is the love of the Spirit in calling the sinner to Christ. The Holy Spirit knocks at the closed door of the heart and waits through all the years of indifference and rebellion and wickedness which He has often to endure. How patient and unceasing His love! How unwilling He is to be grieved away or take His everlasting flight! Some of us He has spent half a century in wooing and winning to the arms of Jesus.

3. *Seen in the New Birth*

The love of the Spirit is seen in the new birth. For, as we have already suggested, the regenerate soul is born of the Spirit and brought forth from the very travailing bosom of this blessed Mother. Real as the pangs of maternal anguish are the sorrows of the maternal Spirit of God over every heart that is laid on the bosom of Jesus.

4. *In Guiding Us*

But not only are we born of the Spirit, but that same gentle Mother becomes the Educator and Guide of our whole life, leading us into all truth, directing us in the way we should go and with maternal tenderness holding our hand and guiding our way through the path of life.

Oh, how gentle and faithful that guiding hand has been! How often it has saved us from perils that we never knew! How we will bless the Holy Spirit when we look backward along the vista of the past in the light of heaven! How we will understand the love of the Spirit then!

5. *Grace in Sanctifying Us*

The love of the Spirit is shown in the grace that He bestows in sanctifying us. Can we ever forget the thrill of joy that sealed our consecration and witnessed to our cleansing from all unrighteousness? That was but the outburst of the love that thrilled His own heart.

6. *In His Indwelling*

The Spirit's love is manifest in His indwelling. He comes to abide in us. He makes our heart His home and sheds abroad the love of God and brings all heaven to fill the sanctuary of the soul.

7. *In His Comforting Influence*

The Spirit's love is seen in His comforting influence. How He cheers the drooping heart, encourages the despondent, wipes away the tears from the mourner's eye and fills us with a joy that we cannot understand! When the heart is ready to sink in bitterness and despair, He is the Joy-bringer and the everlasting Comforter.

8. *In the Power He Gives for Service*

The Spirit's love is seen in the power that He gives us for our service, enduing us with the wisdom and might of Jesus, making our words effective and our lives fruitful and bringing out of the simplest services influences that will last forever.

Everlasting praise and love be unto You, oh, blessed Holy Spirit, for Your boundless everlasting love to us! All we know of Jesus, all we enjoy of the precious gospel we owe to You. You are the life of our life, the joy of our joy, the link that binds us to God and heaven, and the gentle dove whose wings will some day bear our spirits across the void or lift up our forms to meet the Lord in the air. Blessed be the Holy Spirit!

Conclusion

And now, in conclusion, if God is to us Father, Mother, Brother and Bridegroom, let us learn to recognize Him as such. Let us enter into these holy fellowships. Let us lift up every human relationship into divine significance. Let us recognize the earthly, but as a channel to hold the heavenly, as a mirror to reveal the divine, as an alphabet in which to spell out the deeper, closer bonds which God draws us into with Himself.

And if some of our hearts have had to have the

pitcher broken that the light might shine, let it go. The earthly has only perished that we might learn the heavenly. When we have risen from the human to the divine, from the intermediate to the immediate and everlasting, then perhaps God may give back the other without danger of our worshiping the creature more than the Creator.

First let us find "all in God," and then we will be able to "find God in all."

CHAPTER
4

Our Love to God

"The most important [commandment],"
answered Jesus, "is this: . . . 'Love the Lord
your God with all your heart and with all
your soul and with all your mind and with all
your strength.' " (Mark 12:29-30)

A distinguished French preacher, a rationalist, was once invited by a humble, but evangelical minister to preach in his pulpit on this text. He accepted the invitation and the good pastor and his people prayed much that the Lord would bless the sermon to the preacher even more than to the hearers. He was a brilliant and scholarly man who did not believe in the work of Christ except in a rationalistic sense, and so he came with an elaborate discussion of some ethical question suggested by the text. But, as he went on in the sermon, he became evidently confused and moved. After a little while he threw away his manuscript and made a humble confession to his audience, telling them that, while standing there and thinking about these wonderful words, he had been convicted of his own utter sinfulness and helplessness. He had seen something in the light of God of this searching law of love that required his whole heart and soul and mind and strength, of his own utter inability to meet these requirements, and of the worthlessness of all mere human morality or ethical culture to satisfy the imperative and infinite demands of God's perfect law and God's infinite heart. There and then he asked the people to pray for him that he might find an answer to the cry of his heart.

Before that service was ended God was pleased to reveal to him the Lord Jesus Christ as the only answer that could meet his need. He saw Him as the atonement and satisfaction for his wretched failure, and more than this as the Author of the love which he himself could never awaken in his own heart, but which Christ was willing to implant there from His own bosom and to nourish into all fullness of the divine will. He came down from that pulpit an evangelical minister and a saved man, and for many years was one of the devoted and honored leaders of the evangelical church of this country.

In this little incident lies the whole story of the gospel. God's demand of every human being is an infinite love worthy to meet His own, and the only source from which this can ever come is the heart of Christ.

The Law of Love

What God requires of us is love. He is not satisfied with our acceptance of a creed or outward conformity to a law, our mechanical service or our ceremonial worship; He wants our heart and our whole heart. He gives us an infinite love and He demands the same in return. Without this nothing else will satisfy Him; without this the service He asks will be impossible and intolerable.

The only motive adequate for the demands of Christianity is an intense devotion which will find in God the object of our being and the satisfaction of all our desires. The human heart has lost its center; self has become its god; the natural man lives to please himself; the essence of sin is selfishness. And the only antidote to this is a love so exclusive that it leaves no room for any mastery of the heart and life but God alone.

The Philosophy of Love

How can this love be produced in selfish, sinful human hearts? There are tremendous obstacles. In the first place, God is so far distant, so infinitely removed above us, so great and high that we cannot love Him naturally, but are rather oppressed by His majesty and awed by His greatness. Then further, to the natural heart He does not seem attractive, but terrible; His power overawes us and His justice alarms us. He is holy and righteous. But this can only bring us into collision with Him if we are unholy and unrighteous, and the natural heart is full of doubts, fears and guilty apprehensions of His anger and His justice. Such influences are not favorable to love, and, indeed, render it impossible.

There is, still further, the fatal fact that the human heart naturally dreads and hates God. Corrupted by the Fall, it has lost its original confidence and love and there is in it an untamed and instinctive repulsion toward God, just as a hawk and a tiger are naturally wild and ferocious. You can pat a little hawk and an infant tiger all you please and treat them with the tenderest kindness, but they will strike you with instinctive hate the first opportunity. It is part of their nature. So the human heart naturally dreads God; the carnal mind is enmity against God and is not subject to the law of God.

It is evident that before we can meet this divine law of love there must be some extraordinary changes.

First of all, God must reveal Himself to us in His true character and remove the misapprehensions which we feel toward Him. We must see Him as a God of goodness, whose attributes will attract us rather than repel us. And so He has revealed Himself in His gospel, and especially in the character and work of Jesus, as a God of infinite mercy, grace and love. The clouds are melted from His throne and His face shines with the eternal sunlight of infinite beneficence.

Further, we must know that all the causes of separation are removed between Him and us. A guilty conscience must have its fears allayed and be sure that there is no cause for apprehension on account of its guilt, that no stroke of punishment need ever be expected from that divine hand, but that every question has been settled, every sin forgiven and that there is perfect reconciliation and acceptance.

This has been done through the atonement of Christ. The sin has been fully recognized and settled by a sufficient satisfaction and atonement; every penalty has been met by another; and on the most solid foundation an everlasting covenant of peace has been made between God and every sinful man that will accept His love through Jesus Christ.

This is the meaning of the great atonement, or rather, at-one-ment.

This is the meaning of those extraordinary words, "God was reconciling the world to himself in Christ, not counting men's sins against them. And he has committed to us the message of reconciliation. . . . We implore you on Christ's behalf: Be reconciled to God" (2 Corinthians 5:19-20). This is the only basis for the creation of divine love in a human heart.

This must be founded, first, in a knowledge of God in the gospel, and, second, a personal reconciliation to Him through the finished work of Christ.

But there is a third step that God must take. We cannot love one that is very far above us and out of sympathy with us. We must come near to those we love, and they must be able to touch us in personal relationship. A God on Mount Sinai or on the throne of the universe we never can love; He must come nearer to us. The glorious prince who would win the peasant for his bride must come down from his throne and lay aside his royal robes, visit her in disguise in her rustic home. He must meet her in the country lanes and the rural garden and cottage as a neighbor and a friend, before her trembling heart can repose in simple confidence in his affection and meet him, in some sense, as an equal and a friend. And so the great God has come down to us and visited us that He might win our love. The prince of glory has become the little baby of Bethlehem, the man of Galilee, the simple, loving friend who walked among men and women and little children like the rest of us, who was hungry and weary, who suffered often and wept like us, and at last died, was laid in the grave and has become bone of our bone, flesh of our flesh, brother of our race, our own dear Christ.

We can love Him; we cannot help loving Him. He touches us with the finger of a child, with the tenderness of a woman, with the simplicity and sympathy of a human heart. And then when we know that He came from heaven from the very bosom of God; that it was He who made this world and will judge it at the last; when we behold Him stilling the tempest, raising the dead, feeding the multitude with a few loaves and fishes, and proving by His mighty works and His resurrection from the dead that He is indeed the Son of God, oh—He lifts our whole heart right up to heaven. He takes the love we are giving to Him as a man and as a friend and binds it around the very heart and throne of God. Loving Him, we have learned to love God with all our heart and soul and mind and strength. We see our God in the face of Jesus Christ and we hear Him saying to us, "Anyone who has seen me has seen the Father" (John 14:9).

One more thing is wanting. Love must be begotten and nourished by the greatest kindness and affection on the part of its object. We do not merely love people because they are lovely, but we love them because they love us. A very homely person may become extremely dear to us through acts of kindness on his part which awaken all our gratitude and then our tenderest affection. This is true of divine love; we cannot love until we are fully assured of His personal interest in us.

And, therefore, He has taken infinite pains to satisfy us of His regard. Not only has He created us with infinite goodness and provided for us with bountiful care, but, above all, He has redeemed us at infinite cost. The story of redemption is a love letter written in the blood of a human heart, for "God so loved the world that he gave his one and only Son, that whoever believes in him shall not perish but have eternal life" (3:16). Not only has He given Christ to suffer and die for us, but He has shown to each of us personally, the tenderest love, seeking us, calling us, saving us, manifesting to us the deepest kindness and binding us to His heart by 10,000 acts of blessing, so that every Christian can say in grateful remembrance, "We love Him, because He first loved us."

There is still one more divine touch necessary to bring us into the love of God. He Himself must awaken in us the very love that is to meet His own. Indeed He must create it in us and impart it as a new life by putting into us His own very heart. All that we have said about the loveliness and the love of God may be understood and believed, and yet there may be no response from the human heart. We may know that God is only good and kind. We may recognize Him in the person of His Son, coming down to meet us on our own level. We may know that all the barriers between Him and us have been removed by the atonement of His blessed Son. We may be told the story of His eternal love to us and believe it to be true. And yet in the very face of all this portraiture of grace and these tender messages of love, our heart may be as loveless as an iceberg and as incapable of rising to meet Him as that iceberg is to reach the clouds.

In a Scottish pulpit the distinguished and graceful Dr. Blair once said, as he closed his sermon before an admiring audience, "Virtue is a being so lovely that she only needs to be seen to be worshiped." That evening a minister of a different type occupied that pulpit, and, referring to the eloquent passage of the morning, said, "Virtue did come down from heaven in human form and became incarnate in the person of Jesus Christ; and instead of worshiping her the world took that glorious and perfect Man, condemned Him as a malefactor and crucified Him as an outcast of earth and heaven." After all that God has said and done, the human heart is still estranged and must be born again into the love of God before it can return it to Him. Therefore, the blessed Holy Spirit takes the gospel of Jesus and the revelation of His person and applies them to our heart by His quickening touch, so that we do believe and receive the truth and become transformed by it so as to give back God's love again to Him.

Jesus Christ not only comes to us from God bringing to us the Father's love, but He goes back from us to God, uniting Himself with us and enabling us to exercise toward His Father the very same feelings and affections which He Himself has. In a word, He puts His own heart in us and enables us to trust with His trust and love with His love.

Dear friend, would you enter into the love of God? First of all, believe the gospel, the story of the Father's love through the Son. Come to Him as a sinner and receive His mercy and forgiveness and then His quickening Spirit as a free gift, and there will come into your new heart a love which will be born of God, and you will be able to say with a glad response, "We love Him, because He first loved us."

The Life of Love

The Christian's life is a life of love. The first, sweet touch which thrills the forgiven heart is but the beginning of an everlasting experience of a deeper, higher, more divine love. "I pray that you, being rooted and established in love, may have power, together with all the saints, to grasp how wide and long and high and deep is the love of Christ, and to know this love that surpasses knowledge" (Ephesians 3:17-19).

Now, how are we to come into the fullness of this life of love, and how are we to grow in it into all the maturity of the sons of God?

In a general way, it may be said that love is the very substance of sanctification. We never come fully into it until we become wholly sanctified unto God. A newly converted soul has many touches of love, but they are inconstant and intermittent and often succeeded by conflicts, doubts, fears, relapses and experiences of coldness, indifference and spiritual depression and declension. If we would abide in His love, we must learn to abide in Him and to receive Him as our abiding life.

1. The Love He Requires

We must recognize in this new life the kind of love that He requires of us. Much suffering and confusion will be avoided by understanding the real nature of divine love. It is not the mere emotion of pleasurable feeling, the thrill of delightful excitement, a warm gust of ardor and fervor succeeded perhaps by reaction; but it is a great principle.

It really means the voluntary dedication of our whole being to God. It begins with a definite, deliberate choice of God, the decision to be His and His only, to accept His will as the law of our life, and His glory as its great end, and Himself as our joy and portion. So it is really expressed by the act and habit of entire consecration. The love He requires is all your heart, all your soul, all your mind and all your strength (Mark 12:30). This simply means the giving up of all our powers to Him to be possessed by Him and used for His glory. It means the renouncing of our natural will and our willing choice of His will as our highest good, and then the devotion of all the possibilities of our being to Him to be used for the highest purposes of His kingdom and glory.

The man or woman who is living to please himself or herself or others does not know the love of God. "You are the ones who justify yourselves in the eyes of men" (Luke 16:15), Jesus said. "But I know you, I know that you do not have the love of God in your hearts" (John 5:42). You may not have much religious emotion, but if you can truly say, "Every joy of my will and every power of my being are the Lord's and my chief desire is for Him to make the best He can of my life," you are most truly living out the real meaning of the divine law and divine love.

2. *Habitual Standing in Christ*

Remember that love is born of faith and depends upon the habitual recognition of your standing in Christ. Therefore cultivate the constant habit of recognizing yourself as an object of divine love, and say with John, "We know and rely on the love God has for us" (1 John 4:16). Refuse ever to doubt His perfect love for you. No matter what comes to you from your Father, always recognize it as sent in love. Hold firmly to His gracious promise, "I have sworn not to be angry with you, never to rebuke you again" (Isaiah 54:9). Keep yourself in the love of God, looking for the mercy of our Lord Jesus Christ unto eternal life.

Especially remember what the Apostle John has said: "In this way, love is made complete among us so that we will have confidence on the day of judgment, because in this world we are like him" (1 John 4:17). It is thus that our love is made perfect even in the day of judgment, by regarding ourselves in Himself. Our standing is the same as His. The Father looks upon us as He looks upon Him. We stand in His righteousness, in His merits, in His rights, in His purity and even in His love. And so when we see nothing in ourselves to approve and are tempted to think God cannot care for us at all, let us remember God sees us as He sees His dear Son, and loves us even as He loves Him. Immediately our hearts will respond with delight and confidence, and we will know that we are accepted in the Beloved and will have boldness even in the awful day of His coming.

Let us ever stand in Christ. Let us ever present Him to the Father as our Life and as our Representative, and then the love wherewith He loves the Son will be in us, because He is in us.

3. Temperament and Love

Let us recognize the matter of temperament and love according to our nature. Every person does not show love the same way. You may have one little child in your home who is demonstrative, gushing, effusive and always expressing her love. But perhaps she has not the truest heart in your family. There is another little one who says little, but one look from you would break her heart. You will always find her doing little things that others forgot, bearing little sacrifices, showing little kindnesses, perhaps suffering in silence for your sake, and you know that hers is the deepest, truest heart in all your home.

Orpah kissed her mother-in-law, but Ruth clung unto her. And so God has His Ruths and they are often writing hard things against themselves, and saying:

> Lord, it is my chief complaint,
> That my love is weak and faint.

And yet, beloved, what is the real purpose of your life? What is the real outcome of every day? Is God getting the best out of you every moment?

Then perhaps He is saying to you, as He smiles above your tears and fears, "Well done, good and faithful servant!" (Matthew 25:21).

4. *The Intimacies of Life*

Come near to Him and bring Him into all the intimacies of your life if you would grow in His love. You cannot love people at a distance if you want them to touch the most intimate things in your life. If you want to know all the love of Jesus, take Him into your innermost heart and give to Him all the most sacred things in your life. Let Him come into your innermost affection. Let Him search to the core of your very heart. Let Him be the confidant of every thought, the sharer of every joy. Bind Him to your heart by 10,000 little things. Fill up each day with innumerable trifles in which He has a part.

Love is fed more by little things than by great ones. Many a necklace of jewels means less to the receiver than some little flower which a loving hand has plucked for the loved one. Christ is endeared to us by the countless little things we take to Him to do for us. You wake in the night with a chill, you look to Him, and lo! He touches your body with life and healing, and for days the memory of that touch will thrill you with love and gratitude. You lose your keys and do not know where to find them. You search until you are baffled, then you think of asking Him, and in a moment you find them and are extricated from some great embarrassment. And you feel the touch of God as though His presence had been unveiled to you, and for hours the memory of that answered prayer lingers with you. You come to some trying emergency; you are in real peril and you do not know what to do. You look to Him, and again you are not ashamed. Your heart leaps up to heaven with the cry, "Jesus is good to my soul."

These are the ways we grow in His love until, like the banyan tree, which is rooted to the earth, not by one trunk, but by a hundred returning branches which strike into the soil and become new trunks and roots, supporting the vast expanse of spreading branches, so our life becomes rooted in a hundred places to the heart of our God.

5. *Do Little Things*

Better even than this, do little things for Him. The people we love best are the people we do most for. You are most attached to the people that do most for you. The little child that requires constant care is your favorite. The person for whom you have sacrificed most is dearest to you. When Jesus wanted to bind the Samaritan woman to Him, He asked her to give Him a drink of water. When He wanted Abraham to be His friend forever, He asked him to give up his son. Abraham never forgot that he was willing to do it, and God never did either. Perfect and universal obedience is the best test of love. "If you love me," Jesus said, "you will obey what I command" (John 14:15). And again, "You are my friends if you do what I command" (15:14). And again, "This is love for God: to obey his commands" (1 John 5:3).

Once in a while we get a special test, and oh, if we might always meet it so that we ourselves will never have the upbraiding thought that we held anything back from God!

6. *The Atmosphere of Love*

Live in the atmosphere of love. There are different kinds of life. Some people live a life of forms. Their religion consists of ceremonies, observances, things they do and say. Others live a life of intellectual religion. Their religion is largely a creed and doctrine, a set of truths, things they think, sermons they preach or hear, views they hold, principles in which they unite in a testimony for the truth. Others again live a life of duty. Conscience is their predominant quality; obligation is their leading principle. But there is a certain angle and a certain strain about their life. It is true and right, but a little hard and a little negative. Again, others live a life of service. They are chiefly known for the work they do. They are always busy and bustling. Their life is a mass of machinery, perfect, orderly, useful; but lacking repose and sweetness.

The ideal life is the life of love. Christ has put it in a single sentence; "Live in love." It gives a certain complexion, atmosphere, element to our life. You know what a love life means in human relationships. That bride and bridegroom in the early happy days are living a love life. Now we may live such a life with Christ, a life in which His tenderness and our delight in Him will be the predominant elements. We will be ever conscious of a love that has no cloud, no disobedience, no reproof but in which we are conscious every moment that we please Him and that we delight in Him. It is the love life of the Lord. It is the land of Beulah. It is the privilege of the abiding and consecrated child of God. It is the place of the bride, betrothed, robed and waiting for the coming of her Lord, and singing every moment:

> My life is all transfigured with the sweet touch of love,
> On all around there shineth a glory from above;
> The water of earth's pleasure is changed to heavenly wine,
> And life, like Cana's wedding, becomes a feast divine.

7. *Without Thought of Self*

Let our love and life be artless, unconscious, without strain or thought of self. The people who love the most think least about their love and most about the object of it. You ask that wife if she loves her husband and she would be surprised at your question. It never occurred to her to think of her own love. She is thinking rather of him. Ask me if I love Jesus, and I should have to stop and think. I am so absorbed in thinking of Him and being busy for Him that it never occurs to me to look at my own emotions, and if I do I might come into darkness and not be very successful in analyzing them.

It is blessed to love without thinking about it. The most beautiful touch in all the pictures of the rewards of the last day is that place where the righteous answer: "Lord, when did we see you hungry and feed you, or thirsty and give you something to drink?" (Matthew 25:37).

It did not occur to them that they had done anything for Jesus. They had not analyzed their feelings nor been conscious of doing it for Jesus. It was so natural for them to do it for Him that they did it unconsciously and all unconscious things are the most perfect, spontaneous and beautiful.

So let us be filled with His love and it will live itself.

The Claims of Christ upon Our Love

"Do you love me?" the Master asks of each disciple with tender pleading and longing. He expects our first and highest love for Himself, personally, and He has a right to it. More than all our service, more than all our work to build up a cause, is our personal devotion to Him. Mary's gift was precious because it was personal. "You will always have the poor among you, but you will not always have me" (John 12:8), was His tender suggestion of a danger which has often happened since, being more occupied with the work of

Christ than with Christ Himself.

Then we need the love of Christ in order to fit us for His work. Nothing else will give it its true aim and center and nothing else will sustain us amid its pressures. When Jesus was about to send Simon to take care of His flock, He did not ask him. "Do you love my sheep and my lambs?" but it was, "Do you truly love me?" (21:15). Mere love for people will not enable us to be true to them; but love for Christ will give us a reflected love for others that will enable us to touch them from Him and for Him and to bless them as our own direct touch never could.

"Do you truly love me more than these?" He asked Simon. And Simon answered, "Lord, . . . you know that I love you" (21:15). Then Jesus said, "Feed my lambs" (21:15). "Do you truly love me?" (21:16), He asked again. And Simon answered again, somewhat grieved, "Yes, Lord, you know that I love you" (21:16). Then Jesus gave a second commission, "Take care of my sheep" (21:16). And now a third time He asked, taking up Peter's stronger word, "Do you love me?" (21:17). Peter answered with all his heart, "Lord, you know all things; you know that I love you" (21:17). And then Jesus answered with the third commission, "Feed my sheep" (21:17). These three delicate trusts—the feeding of the lambs, the children and the newly saved, the shepherding of the feeble wanderer and back-slider and the nurturing of the stronger sheep—need, as their inspiration and motive, not so much love for the sheep and lambs as love for the One who owns them. Oh! If we love Him we will love His own far better than any human preference or sentiment can enable us to love.

If we go to our work from the bosom of the Master, we will not lack the tenderness and sympathy, the unction and passionate love of souls that will draw them, not to us, but to Him, and touch them, not with our sympathy, but with His great love. As the moon shines with the reflected light of the sun, so all other love must come from the love of Jesus if it would be true, lasting and effectual.

Conclusion

There is a very solemn passage in the closing sentence of one of Paul's letters that may well sum up the practical truths which we have been considering: "If anyone does not love the Lord— a curse be on him. Come, O Lord!" (1 Corinthians 16:22), which means accursed at the coming of the Lord. We may well pause and ask, or rather ask the Lord to ask us, "Do I love the Lord Jesus Christ?"

He is so worthy of our love that if we are found indifferent or unloving the whole universe will echo our sentence, and our own hearts will feel and know that it is deserved. Not to love such a friend is a sin which, even we ourselves, never can forgive.

He will not ask you then what you did for His cause, what you gave for missions, what you said in His name, what you believe about His Word, but how much you loved Him.

It is a very awful fact that in the two last letters of Jesus from heaven to His church, the lack of love is marked with solemn emphasis as the ground for the rejection of two of these churches. The church of Ephesus had much orthodoxy, much work, much zeal, much patience, and He could say,

> I know your deeds, your hard work and your perseverance. I know that you cannot tolerate wicked men, that you have tested those who claim to be apostles but are not, and have found them false. . . .
> Yet I hold this against you: You have forsaken your first love. . . . Repent and do the things you did at first. If you do not repent, I will come to you and remove your lampstand from its place. (Revelation 2:2, 4-5)

And the church in Laodicea, the last of the seven, had no other fault than this, that she was lukewarm, and neither cold nor hot, and for that inexcusable offense He was about to reject her altogether (3:14-23).

Oh, beloved, ask God to search your heart to see how much of your Christian life and work has its root in real love to Jesus.

Long ago that saintly man, John Flavel, preached a sermon on this same text, "If any man love not the Lord Jesus, let him be accursed." He was about to pronounce the benediction, when he suddenly paused, and with hands uplifted and with many tears, said, very solemnly, "How can I bless whom God hath cursed." Then he added, "There is someone here on whom this curse must rest." There was one man in that congregation, a young man of 25, who was deeply touched with this solemn warning. He went away from the church and wandered around the world until at last he reached South America, where he spent many years and lived to be a very old man. One day, when 100 years old, he stumbled into a chapel and heard a minister preach from the text in Isaiah, "The sinner being one hundred years old shall be accursed." Suddenly the memory of the message of John Flavel rushed across his mind. It had been 75 years ago, but seemed like the voice from the judgment of Christ. He trembled and broke completely down in anguish and despair. He sought the minister with scarcely a hope in his heart. It seemed like the knell of doom. He was just 100 years old and the curse seemed sealed forever. But God let the light fall into the old man's heart, and he was saved and the curse was turned into a blessing.

Oh that today, even this parting word may save some soul from meeting it again in that last day as a lightning arrow of judgment and condemnation!

CHAPTER
5

The New Commandment

Love your neighbor as yourself. (Mark 12:31)

Love does no harm to its neighbor. Therefore love is the fulfillment of the law. (Romans 13:10)

So in everything, do to others what you would have them do to you, for this sums up the Law and the Prophets. (Matthew 7:12)

Yet I am writing you a new command; its truth is seen in him and you. (1 John 2:8)

A new command I give you: Love one another. As I have loved you, so you must love one another. (John 13:34)

These various passages lead us on through a progression of truths of the most profound and practical importance.

The Old Testament Law of Love

In the book of Deuteronomy we have a number of commentaries on the moral law as given by Moses. During the wanderings in the wilderness for 40 years Moses again and again expounded the meaning of that great law. He taught the children of Israel in many practical addresses the great principle of righteousness which God had summed up in those 10 words which we call the Decalogue [the Ten Commandments]. And in some of these addresses we have a beautiful exposition of the great law of love to God and man. There is nothing in modern ethics comparable with the beautiful precepts of this ancient code. Our social and civil laws are put to shame by the large and generous provisions of the statutes of Deuteronomy. Let us look at a few examples:

> If you see your brother's ox or sheep straying, do not ignore it but be sure to take it back to him. If the brother does not live near you or if you do not know who he is, take it home with you and keep it until he comes looking for it. Then give it back to him. . . .
>
> If you see your brother's donkey or his ox fallen on the road, do not ignore it. Help him get it to its feet. (22:1-2, 4)

What a beautiful illustration these words are of the law of love between neighbor and neighbor!

Then in the sixth and seventh verses, what a touch of God's tenderness even to the lower animals: "If you come across a bird's nest beside the road, either in a tree or on the ground, and the mother is sitting on the young or on the eggs, do not take the mother with the young. You may take the young, but be sure to let the mother go, so that it may go well with you and you may have a long life."

It was not forbidden to capture the young birds if they were needed for any proper purpose, but in no case must they be left motherless.

Then verse eight is a good deal in advance of our building laws: "When you build a new house, make a parapet around your roof so that you may not bring the guilt of bloodshed on your house if someone falls from the roof."

Again in 23:8 we have the original of the fugitive slave law. And verse 19 would revolutionize our civil laws: "Do not charge your brother interest, whether on money or food or anything else that may earn interest."

Again, in the last verses of chapter 23, we have a check upon the selfishness of the farmer: "If you enter your neighbor's vineyard, you may eat all the grapes you want, but do not put any in your basket. If you enter your neighbor's grainfield, you may pluck kernels with your hands, but you must not put a sickle to his standing grain" (23:24-25).

There is nothing more beautiful in the Bible than the provisions made for restoring pledges taken for debt. No pledge must be taken which was necessary to the life of the owner, such as his millstone; and if the pledge was necessary for the man's comfort at night it must be restored until the morning:

> When you make a loan of any kind to your neighbor, do not go into his house to get what he is offering as a pledge. Stay outside and let the man to whom you are making the loan bring the pledge out to you. If the man is poor, do not go to sleep with his pledge in your possession. Return his cloak to him by sunset, so that he may sleep in it. Then he will thank you, and it will be regarded as a righteous act in the sight of the LORD your God. (24:10-13)

Even the newly married wife was protected by the tender and generous conditions of the ancient law of love: "If a man has recently married, he must not be sent to war or have any other duty laid on him. For one year he is to be free to stay at home and bring happiness to the wife he has married" (24:5).

Even the punishment of the wicked must be moderate: "He must not give him more than forty lashes. If he is flogged more than that, your brother will be degraded in your eyes" (25:3).

Yes, the very cattle must be allowed to eat as they walk over the corn on the threshing floor:

"Do not muzzle an ox while it is treading out the grain" (25:4).

After all that has been said about the cruelty of Judaism and its law, there are a good many things in the above statutes that our boasted American civilization might well copy.

Christ's New Edition of the Old Testament Law of Love

Our Lord has given us in His incomparable teachings a striking and beautiful epitome of this ancient law: "So in everything, do to others what you would have them do to you, for this sums up the Law and the Prophets" (Matthew 7:12).

The remarkable thing connected with this verse is the pointed and personal way in which it brings this law home to every man's heart and conscience and awakens in him a principle searching enough to compel him to the practice of this precept, even for his own self-interest. It carries with it the constant admonition that we ourselves will be treated as we treat others. There is a strange and solemn law running through the Word of God and His providence which we find expressed in this tremendous sentence in the book of Ezekiel. "I will even deal with thee as thou hast done" (16:59, KJV). The golden rule which Jesus gave was based upon that principle. It sends every man forth to act on the assumption that he, by his treatment of his brother, is practically deciding his own destiny.

Nothing touches a man so much as his own interest; that is, a natural man. Right and wrong, humanity and benevolence may seem small things when they affect another, but when they come home to our own life they grow strangely real. It was a small matter for Adonibezek, the cruel Canaanite chieftain, to cut off the toes and fingers of 70 kings, but when it came back to his own person, and he found his own toes and fingers dismembered, then he remembered, with strange vividness, the anguish of the men that he had tortured and recognized the just retribution of the law of love.

Now God would have us just change the direction of this a little and look forward to it rather than backward. And as we speak of a brother or act to a neighbor be ready to ask ourselves, "Am I prepared to receive the same treatment? Do I now conscientiously and willingly choose this very thing for myself?" Shall we henceforth act on this assumption and remember that we are content that God will do for us the thing that we do for others? Oh, that our life may be filled with such blessing that the return of our actions will bring only blessing to us. There is a strange mechanical toy, which, when you throw it into the air, describes an ellipse and comes back to you again. Beloved, we are throwing constantly just such influences from us. Let us walk through life remembering that our actions to others are on their way back to alight on our own heads. As we act from this principle we will be able, at least, to reach in some measure the spirit of justice if not of love.

Now this is not the highest plane; this is simply morality and legality, but it is a great way in advance of the Christianity of some people. Christ re-enacted this old law and it is binding upon us as the very lowest plane of Christian ethics.

The New Testament Law of Love

Jesus has given us a law of love quite distinct from this and as far beyond it as the heavens are above the earth. It is this: "A new command I give you: Love one another. As I have loved you, so you must love one another" (John 13:34). The Old Testament law is, "Love your neighbor as yourself" (Leviticus 19:18). The New Testament law is, "Love one another more than you love yourself, even as I loved you"; for Christ so loved us that He gave Himself for us; and the Apostle John has added: "This is how we know what love is: Jesus Christ laid down his life for us. And we ought to lay down our lives for our brothers" (1 John 3:16).

It was these two laws that John had in mind when he said: "I am not writing you a new command but an old one, which you have had since the beginning" (2:7). That is the Old Testament law of love. But then he adds again: "Yet I am writing you a new command; its truth is seen in him and you, because the darkness is passing and the true light is already shining" (2:8). Now this is the New Testament law of love which he expresses by saying that it is true in Him and in you. That is but another version of the saying,

"As I have loved you."

Now, it is hardly necessary to say that on the very first view of the matter there is a radical and infinite difference between the Old Testament and the New. The teaching of Jesus Christ is way in advance of the teaching of Moses. Christ always recognized the teaching of Moses, confirmed it, re-enacted it, but He went much farther. Look, for example, at two cases:

Centuries ago a holy prophet, named Zechariah, was stoned to death between the temple and the altar by command of a king of Israel. Jesus Himself refers to it with severest condemnation of the crime and honors him as one of the first of the martyr prophets. But as he died, do you remember what he said? Looking up to heaven for vindication and vengeance, he cried, "May the LORD see this and call you to account" (2 Chronicles 24:22). And most terribly did God require it from his wicked murderers.

But look at another scene. Another servant of God lies bleeding under a heap of stones at the hands of his murderers. It is the holy Stephen, the first Christian martyr, and as the blood oozes from his wounds and the life fades from his breath, what does he say? Looking up into the opening heaven he cries, with a face all lit up with the love of his Master, "Lord, do not hold this sin against them" (Acts 7:60). These two pictures, as with a flash of celestial light, reveal the true spirit of Judaism and Christianity. The one was justice, the other is love. The one was a true step in the revelation of God, but only a step; the other is the completion and consummation of the whole in the revelation of that love of which justice is but one of the foundation stones.

Look at the treatment of the enemies of the Israelites by Moses and Joshua; it was just, but it was terribly severe. But look at the last acts and words of Jesus Christ as He weeps over Jerusalem that was about to crucify Him, and with His last breath intercedes upon the cross for the men that were crucifying Him, "Father, forgive them, for they do not know what they are doing" (Luke 23:34). This is the law of love which rises above Mount Sinai, even as the ascension glory is higher than the grandeur and terror of the Mount of Fire. Two things are involved in this New Testament law:

1. The Very High Standard

The highest standard was set: "As I have loved you" (John 13:34). You are to love your neighbor with no less love than that of God Himself. You are to think of him as God thinks of him, to treat him as God treats him, to love him as Christ loves him. No, love him as Christ loves *you*, for He does not even leave it for you to judge how much Christ may love him, but just as you want Him to love you so you must love your neighbor. Now do not try to lower this standard. Do not say it is impracticable and impossible. Even if you never reach it, even if you feel that no man has reached it or can reach it, keep it: "Let God be true and every man a liar." There must be some way of fulfilling it or God never would have given it as His divine law. Let us keep the standard on its highest level and ask God to somehow let us reach it.

2. *The Sources and Means*

The law also implies in its very terms the sources and means through which we may fulfill it. The words "As I" suggest the great secret. It is not only like Him but through Him and by Him that we are enabled to love. The Apostle John hinted at this in the verse already quoted, "I am writing you a new command; its truth is seen in him and you, because the darkness is passing and the true light is already shining" (1 John 2:8). Now it is true in Him first and thus in you. It is true in you because He is in you. In a word, Christ Himself must do the loving in us, and the secret of it is abiding in Him.

It is just the same secret of sanctification. It is the old story; the life of holiness is the life of love, and the secret of holiness is the indwelling life of Christ. We must come up to it and find our helplessness. Often we must go through the sad and humbling experience of trying ourselves. Then, bruised, baffled, ready to sink in despair, convicted in our conscience of the imperative necessity of love, and yet, convinced of our utter inability to give it, we fall helpless at His feet. And then He Himself comes and breathes in us His own love, puts in us His own heart and enables us to love in Him and like Him, and to say with rejoicing hearts, "The life I live in the body, I live by faith in the Son of God, who loved me and gave himself for me" (Galatians 2:20).

The Application of This Great Law to Our Various Relationships

1. Our Love to the Brethren

Our nearest human relationship is to the children of God. We are to love them as we cannot love the world—even as Christ loves them, with the peculiar love that others cannot share. "Love one another," is His command, "as I have loved you" (John 13:34). There is a great mystery in the body of Christ; the Church which is separated, called and sanctified as His Bride, is, if fitly framed together, intimately connected with our life. We will have to speak of this more fully elsewhere. But at present it is enough to say that our life and blessing greatly depend on our relationships one to the other. And it, when "joined and held together by every supporting ligament, grows and builds itself up in love, as each part does its work" (Ephesians 4:16).

You cannot have a strong, healthy and progressive Christian life unless you are rightly adjusted to your brothers and sisters and living in love to every one of them. This love is part of our common life. We love them instinctively because they are part of us and we of them. We do not love them because of their natural qualities nor because they are dear to us through relationship or kind offices toward us, but we love them because they are Christ's. "Anyone who receives a righteous man because he is a righteous man will receive a righteous man's reward. And if anyone gives even a cup of cold water to one of these little ones because he is my disciple, I tell you the truth, he will certainly not lose his reward" (Matthew 10:41-42). The principle of love here is, as already expressed, "Love one another. As I have loved you" (John 13:34).

It is not a natural affection, but a divine love, the heart of Christ going out from us to our brethren, the love of God reflected from us upon them. We do not love their persons, but we recognize the love of Christ in them. The Christ in us meets the Christ in them, and life touches life and God meets God. This will help us through the hard places in the life of love. Think how Jesus feels toward your brother, and then ask Him to give you His thought and feeling, and you will not find it hard to love. Think how Jesus feels to you and loves you. Think how you want Him to love you and then measure your love to your brother by this. How does Christ regard your faults? As you would have Him regard them, so regard your brother's.

Jesus is not looking at you as you are in yourself, but He is looking at you robed in His grace, and thinking of you ever as you shall be when He has finished in you His glorious work and when you are like Him in the eternal future. So think of your brother, not in his present imperfection, but as he shall be after the finished work of divine grace. Anticipate the future, foredate the coming glory, rise to the heavenly realities, receive people as you will receive them in heaven, and faith and hope will become handmaids to love. And with the heart and eyes of Jesus you will look out on all around you, and earth will become heaven and the most uncongenial people will be altogether lovely.

2. Our Friends and Relatives

The same principle will apply to our love for those who are naturally dear to us and linked with us by the ties of peculiar affection or kindred bonds, where earthly loves must be transformed into heavenly fellowships. We have a symbol of this in the story of Isaac. Naturally he was very dear to Abraham, spiritually doubly dear because he was God-given and God-linked. He was the channel through whom all Abraham's hopes and blessings were to come, and yet that natural love, and even that spiritual love, had to be crucified and given back from the dead in resurrection life. So Isaac was offered up, the same as dead, and then when he came back to Abraham he was not the old Isaac any more, but a type of the resurrection, the child of a heavenly love and hope— God's Isaac rather than his, but doubly his because God's. And so all our friendships must be first surrendered and then received with the touch of heaven.

Therefore, Paul says in Ephesians, with respect to the tenderest of human bonds, "Husbands, love your wives, just as Christ loved the church and gave himself up for her" (5:25). Do not love them merely with a natural affection, but let Christ put in you His own divine love and make your marriage a symbol of the eternal union with the Lord Himself. So again he says to fathers, "do not exasperate your children; instead, bring them up in the training and instruction of the Lord" (6:4). That is, treat them as the Lord treats you, love them as the Lord loves you, train them as the Lord trains you. And so, on the other hand, the children are to obey their parents as unto the Lord. So we find every human relationship is to touch and to receive a new light and life from its fellowship with the divine. Thus every earthly thing will become a sacrament and will speak to us of the divine and the eternal.

3. Our Enemies

The highest kind of love is love for those who hurt us. The ethics of the world have never reached anything approachable to Christ's command, "Love your enemies, do good to those who hate you, bless those who curse you, pray for those who mistreat you" (Luke 6:27-28). And the pattern and motive of this is: "your Father in heaven . . . causes his sun to rise on the evil and the good, and sends rain on the righteous and the unrighteous" (Matthew 5:45). "Be perfect, therefore," He adds with special reference to this, "as your heavenly Father is perfect" (5:48).

In the portraiture of love given us in the thirteenth chapter of First Corinthians, it is very touching and beautiful to observe that the first and last touches in the picture are touches of sorrow. As the heavenly figure comes before us and begins her beautiful advance, she is suffering, "Love is patient" (13:4). And after the long, sad way, as she passes out of sight to her crown, the tears are still in her eyes, the chastened sorrow is still upon her face, but illuminated with a light all beautiful and divine, and the last word that the recording angel speaks of her is "[Love] always perseveres" (13:7). She begins and ends her way with long-suffering patience.

When the heart is stung with a sense of wrong, injustice, misrepresentation and cruel hate, nothing but the very power of supernatural grace can enable us to love those who wrong us and bless those who hate us. We can only do it through the Christ in us. It is the same principle as "I have loved you." It is the spirit of Him who hung on the tree re-echoing in us His own cry, "Father, forgive them, for they do not know what they are doing" (Luke 23:34). How could He love them? Well, He saw their side of it, He saw the sorrow that was coming to them, He saw them plunged in anguish and pursued with vengeance from which He could not save them, and He could only weep over them. And then He saw Himself crowned with glory, all the richer and the grander because of His present sorrows, and He would not keep back if He could a single blood-drop nor a single tear, but "for the joy set before him endured the cross, scorning its shame" (Hebrews 12:2).

If we will look at things that way we can love them too.

4. Love for the Wicked and Unworthy

Next, we must love the wicked and unworthy. I do not mean now those who do us wrong, but those who without personally affecting us yet are to us repulsive, uncongenial and are deservedly so—the impure, unjust, the selfish, the drunkard, the profligate, the heathen. How can we love these? On the same principle, "Even as He" (1 John 2:6). "For God so loved the world that he gave his one and only Son" (John 3:16). "Because of his great love for us, God, who is rich in mercy, made us alive with Christ even when we were dead in transgressions" (Ephesians 2:4-5). "But God demonstrates his own love for us in this: While we were still sinners, Christ died for us" (Romans 5:8). And if the heart of God is in us we will love the sinful, the vile, the unlovely.

That is the meaning of that strange affection which in many souls becomes a passion all-constraining and consuming—the love of souls. It was this that made Paul willing almost to sacrifice his own soul if he might save his countrymen. It was this that inspired the preaching of Whitfield and made Rutherford cry, "Your salvation would be ten salvations to me, your heaven ten heavens to me." It is this which sends the lady of culture and sensitivity, with the very ecstasy of love, down into the slums. It is this that makes it, literally, a joy to throw her arms about her fallen sister covered with vermin and disease, and kiss her with the pure, fresh love that only a saintly soul can give, and, literally, love her to Christ. It is this which enables us to take hold of people whom we do not even know and pray for them and reach out to grasp their very souls as with a mother's travailing love. How can we have it? Only as God Himself gives it to us and as Christ fully lives in us.

A young friend said to me once, "I do not seem to have a special call to speak to the unsaved. I find much more freedom in talking to Christians and teaching them. And I wonder often if I am really to be a foreign missionary, or am mistaking my calling and should rather labor among the churches at home." I could only say, "No, sister, do not try to adapt yourself to your feeling, but bring your feeling up to His own example." Jesus, who was the most marvelous Teacher of the disciples, was the one that loved best to stand among the lost. His heart so yearned over them that we can say of Him, "This man lives for sinners." Scripture tells us, "Now the tax collectors and 'sinners' were all gathering around to hear him" (Luke 15:1). If the Christ heart is full in us we will be found with the Good Shepherd seeking the one who has gone astray until we find him. Let us be suspicious of our spiritual condition if we have not a fresh, tender love for souls. God is able to give it and to keep it.

5. *Touches the Entire World*

Finally, this love will touch all the world and cover us with a mantle of universal charity. We will walk among men representing God to them, thinking and feeling for them even as Jesus would.

The great principle is in these two little words, "As I."

Oh, what a sacred, solemn trust, that while He is representing us in heaven, we may represent Him here. We must touch men for Him, and make them feel as we pass by as if God had for a moment touched their lives and heaven had opened its crystal portals and let one ray of its eternal light fall upon their dark path. Oh, this is our high honor, beloved, to go about the city a little while longer, to pass up and down the streets, to move through the home, and the store, and the church, representing God to men, thinking of them and feeling for them as He does, and recognizing it as our great trust to make them think of God by seeing us.

God wants everybody to have an eternal memory of something sweet and beautiful. He wants even the poor sinner to be without excuse about knowing the love of God. And if he cannot see it in Jesus, let him see it in you. Some day the memory of that little ray of light may bring him to the Savior too.

And now, in conclusion, how can we have God's love to people?

There are two simple conditions.

First, will you choose, instead of your own selfishness, your own willfulness, your own passion, your own vindication, your desire for revenge or satisfaction, will you let that little thing go and choose instead to love the people whom you would rather not love, and to love them even as He loves you?

And second, will you choose to love all-round? You cannot have love in one or two directions and then hate in the others. If you have God, you must have the perfect circle. The sinner would like to have his sins forgiven, to be saved from drunkenness and self-destruction; but he does not want to give up some of the pleasant sins. But God does not want to have him on those terms; he must be wholly saved or not at all. Christ will not pardon one sin and leave another. If you are willing to have His complete forgiveness and cleansing and His full salvation, you can have it; but if you only want what pleases you, you cannot have anything. And so it is with love. If you will have an all-round love, and enter into the heart of God without reserve, then you can have it, and Christ will take possession of that surrendered will and breathe in you His own affections, desires and nature, and you will be in this world, "Even as He."

One in Him

> *That all of them may be one, Father, just as you are in me and I am in you. May they also be in us so that the world may believe that you have sent me. . . . and have loved them even as you have loved me. (John 17:21-23)*

This is Christ's last prayer for His beloved disciples. It must be very dear to His heart. Its fulfillment was the glory of the Apostolic Church. The worst enemies of Christianity were compelled to concede the love of the early disciples, and they attributed the success of Christianity chiefly to this cause. The decline of Christian unity and the growth of sectarianism have marked the declension of true Christianity. And the glorious signs of deeper unity among the consecrated children of God are among the most hopeful signs today of the near approach of the Lord's return, and of the blessed time when we will all be made perfect in one, and the world will believe that Christ is the Sent One.

The two beautiful parables of the Treasure and the Pearl are prophetic of the progress of the Church. The former represents believers in their individuality, the latter the Church in its unity. The Treasure is the many; the Pearl is the One. At present we are like the scattered treasure hid in the field; but the Lord is gathering us together, and soon the Body of Christ will be united in the glory of the Bride and will shine in the millennial age like a cluster of crystals and jewels, as John beheld the vision in his glorious Apocalypse.

There is an old legend that once in Eden there was a beautiful temple of jewels. It was the sanctuary where man met with God, and it was the symbol of the unity of His children with Himself. It was the paragon of Eden and of earth. Its dome was a flashing diamond. Its windows were rubies, emeralds and amethysts. Its floor was paved with gold. Its doors were brilliant with surpassing beauty. But in the rupture that followed the fall of man, the temple was wrecked and scattered in fragments throughout the world so that pieces of it are now found in rocks and mountains and riverbeds, in the precious jewels of the mine which men are gathering and wearing for their adornment. But the old legend tells us that the fragments are yet to be gathered together, and in the coming age the temple is to be built once more with a grander glory even than in the primeval morning of the world.

All this is true, anyhow, in the spiritual world. That temple of spiritual gems was once the sanctuary of the Church of God. Such a beautiful house of almost spotless purity and unbroken unity was the early Church in the upper room. But alas, the vision has been defaced, the temple has been riven into fragments, and the fragments are scattered now in every part of the Church of God. Christian life and character today are only seen in their fullness in individuals, and the picture of the complete unity of the Apostolic Church is nowhere to be found.

A hundred denominations based on human creeds and following human leaders divide up the army of the living God, and any single section is but a very narrow and partial expression of the glorious plan given to us in the New Testament. Some of us have tried to have an ideal church. We have prayed for it. We have suffered for it. We have labored for it. We have wept over it. But we have seen our brightest dreams blasted by the worldliness and selfishness of unsanctified men. And we have felt that all we could do was simply to gather individual fragments and to prepare the materials piece by piece and that by-and-by somewhere else we should see them framed together and a glorious temple arise in its millennial light and loveliness.

Yes, the temple will be rebuilt, the scattered jewels will be reunited, and brighter than 10,000 suns shall be the glory of the new Jerusalem when it shall descend from heaven, flashing in all the radiance of the ruby and the rainbow, and embodying all the glory of its Architect and Head.

But, as far as possible, let us realize the vision here. The Master did not mean it all for that coming age. Before He comes again it will be largely fulfilled in a real Body on earth. Not perhaps in human organizations, but, at least, in a deep spiritual fellowship that will realize in some measure His glorious conception.

The Meaning of Christian Unity

1. One in Him

We are one in Him, our Head, "That all of them may be one, Father, just as you are in me and I am in you. May they also be in us" (John 17:21).

We are united to each other by being united to Him. We do not establish our relationship first with each other, but first with Him, and then through Him with one another. The little birdlings press close to the mother's breast, and necessarily, therefore, close to each other. The spokes of the wheel fasten into the hub and touch each other there, because they all touch the center. The children of the family live together and look alike because they all come from one parental fountain of life and lie on one maternal breast.

Therefore, there can be no unity apart from Christ. We cannot love people by trying to love them. But if we both love Him, we will love each other in consequence. Therefore, there can be no unity on the part of those who do not believe in Him. Organization will not make us one; common principles will not make us one. But if we are united to Him, then we cannot but touch each other.

In a foreign city three ministers of different languages met. They could not speak to each other except one word, but they looked into each other's eyes. Then they all pronounced together the one word, "Jesus," and their hands clasped and their tears flowed and they felt that they were one.

Not only do we derive our unity from Him, but He is the pattern of it. We are to be one even as the Father and the Son are one. The Divine Trinity is a pattern of the Church of God. It is a very solemn and tremendous thought. Just as the Godhead is one, so should we be. Think what an awful thing it would be for the Father and Son for a moment to separate. Think what a blasphemy it would be even to think of a disagreement or a difference there. And then think what an awful thing it must be for Christians to be divided. It is as important that we should be one as that God should be one. Will you remember, beloved, the next time the enemy seeks to rend you from the Body of Christ or to use you to rend the Body of Christ that you are to stand to your brother even as the Son to His Father?

2. *One in a Common Life*

We are one in a common life. It is the oneness of nature. You might harness a tiger and a lamb together, but they would never work in unity.

You might educate and train a hawk and a dove, but they never would be able to do anything but devour each other. They have not the same nature; you cannot make them coalesce. And so you cannot have unity between the natural heart and the regenerated spirit. "What harmony is there between Christ and Belial? What does a believer have in common with an unbeliever? . . . Therefore come out from them and be separate, says the Lord" (2 Corinthians 6:15, 17).

The greatest hindrance to Christian unity in the Church is the number who belong to the Church and do not believe in Christ. They have not the same nature. It is like filling a cage with hawks and doves. So long as the Church is made up of unholy men and women who are living for their own pleasure and ambition, it will be a divided church. It will be like Daniel's vision of the image, partly iron and partly clay, and it cannot stand.

3. *One in Truth*

We are one in the truth. There must be, first, unity of life, and then, unity of truth. The divine order is not to draw up a creed and to adopt a platform of principles and then live up to them, but it is to receive a new birth and then believe the truth as a living experience. Unity of doctrine is very blessed if we have first unity of experience. The more complete our agreement of mind, the more intimate will be our unity of heart, if we have learned the true life to begin with.

We can all remember how delightful it was when first we saw Christ as our Savior, to find someone else who believed as we did and had the same experience. To meet a Christian in some far-off land among strangers thrilled all our hearts with a delightful home feeling and a sense of oneness.

Some of us can remember later in our life when we came to know Him as Sanctifier, and the blessed truth that Jesus Christ can cleanse and keep the heart in perfect peace and purity became a personal experience. How lonely we felt even among Christians who did not believe this, and how well we remember the first time we met someone who felt as we did and believed as we did! How a second chord was added to our harmony and our whole being responded with a touch of deeper unity! It was an instrument of two strings now.

And then we came to know Him in a still deeper intimacy as our Healer. But none of our friends believed it. Even our consecrated friends thought we went too far, and we stood alone under the reproach of fanaticism. But when we heard a trembling voice repeating the same testimony, our whole heart thrilled with fellowship, and we recognized a nearer brother. There was a third chord in our instrument of many strings; there was a deeper harmony; there was a fuller chorus of love and oneness.

And then there came the crowning revelation of Jesus as our coming Lord. Beyond all the blessings of the present we saw the glorious hope of His appearing. We believed it as a doctrine and we accepted it as a personal hope. We came under its living experience. We rejoiced in it. We felt it was ours. But we found few who believed it. We longed for fellowship and sympathy. And as the years have gone by we have been picking out people who believe this truth and they seem nearer to us. They seem to be with us the members of an inner family circle preparing together for some glorious day when we will stand in His likeness together and be welcomed at the marriage of the Lamb.

It is a fourfold unity; it is a harmony without a discord. Thank God, it is the blessed platform on which many of us stand and in which we have a oneness that others cannot understand, in Christ our Savior, Healer and coming Lord.

4. One in the Holy Spirit

We are one in the Holy Spirit. "For we were all baptized by one Spirit into one body—whether Jews or Greeks, slave or free" (1 Corinthians 12:13).

It is only in so far as we are in the Spirit that we can be one. We cannot touch the human in people; we must feel for and find the Holy Spirit in others. The Holy Spirit in us will meet the Spirit in them. Therefore, in times of great revival and profound spiritual blessing there is always much unity. The barriers of sectarianism are swept away. The grievances of years are healed.

The heart of God's people swells and flows together and is enlarged. And the spirit of Apostolic Christianity is in some measure realized once more.

Walking along the beach you can see many little pools when the tide is out. Each is a little ocean to itself, with perhaps a few little fish floating in their pond and feeling their importance. But when the tide comes in, all these little pools are flooded into one great ocean and the selfish little lake goes out to sea and finds itself lost in an infinite largeness of which it becomes a part. And all the little fish find themselves in fellowship with one another and become lost amid the greater creatures that they meet in the mighty ocean.

So when men build a church on mere human lines they go into sects and sections; they become absorbed in their own self-importance and they look askance at one another. But when the floods of the Holy Spirit sweep in, all this is changed. Selfishness is melted away and every little ecclesiastical circle gets broadened into a larger fellowship, and men begin to see how small they are in the larger things which are opened to their vision. The great remedy, therefore, for sectarianism is the baptism of the Holy Spirit and the restoration of the power of primitive Christianity.

Not only does the Holy Spirit give the bond of unity, but He also gives us the full enduement which completes the power of the Church and fits her for her work. It is not enough for the members to touch each other in perfect accord, but it is necessary also that the Church as a whole will be equipped for her great work with all the gifts and graces of the Spirit, and that she will present to the world a united front not only of harmony, but also of power and glory. "Fair as the moon, bright as the sun, majestic as the stars in procession" (Song of Songs 6:10). Therefore, the Holy Spirit has provided for the Church a great variety of ministries, operations and gifts, that she may stand equipped for her great calling in all the fullness of God's power.

The complete unity of the Church requires that all these gifts and graces be in constant operation. They are like the robes of a fair woman or the features of her face—the absence of one destroys the unity of expression. The Apostolic Church was arrayed in all the glory of the Spirit and fully represented Christ to the world without a mutilated member or a lacking enduement. The modern church retains but a few fragments of this primeval array and stands with tattered garments and rent girdle, a spectacle of humiliation, oftentimes, before the world to which her Lord has sent her to represent not only His mercy, but also His kingly power.

5. One in Spiritual Fellowship

We are one in spiritual fellowship. It is not enough that we have one life; it must be expressed in mutual love, communion, prayer and help. And, therefore, God had provided for the communion of saints. This is maintained not only by outward acts of worship and fellowship, but also by inward sympathies and mutual intercessions which could not be expressed in any outward form. Probably when we reach the perfect life we will not need the medium of speech to express our thoughts and feelings, but heart to heart, even as we understand Him now, we will meet in the intuitions of the Spirit, and know, even as we are known. In a sense and measure, we may anticipate this here. There is a fellowship of heart and prayer which the Holy Spirit can give beyond all power of speech. God can lay upon us our brother's or our sister's need and enable us to stand with them before the throne when there is no outward communication whatever. Across wide oceans and vast continents heart can touch heart and meet before the throne, and we can bring blessings down upon the heads of those we never met.

God would have us so adjusted, so sensitive, so fitly framed together that we will know His voice in this respect and always be able to catch the spirit of His prayer and respond to the faintest hint from the throne. Oh, how many a sorrow might be lightened, how many a life might be saved if we were ever obedient to the voice of the Spirit's prayer! He wants to have us like an Eolian harp that does not need the touch of fingers, but only the breath of God to bring out its harmonies. The Apostle Paul knew this and could say, "Who is weak, and I do not feel weak? Who is led into sin, and I do not inwardly burn?" (2 Corinthians 11:29). And he has said to us in another place, "Carry each other's burdens, and in this way you will fulfill the law of Christ" (Galatians 6:2). There is a deep and real meaning in these words, "If you have any encouragement from being united with Christ, if any comfort from his love, if any fellowship with the Spirit, if any tenderness and compassion, then make my joy complete by being like-minded, having the same love, being one in spirit and purpose" (Philippians 2:1-2).

Do we know this fellowship in the Spirit? Do we know this tenderness and compassion? Not hooks of steel as human poetry had rudely expressed it, but cords of human heart strings and of divine sympathy—these are the bonds that bind us together.

> We share our mutual woes,
>   Our mutual burdens bear;
> And often for each other flows,
>   The sympathizing tear.

6. *One in Cooperation and Service*

We are one in cooperation and service. How much of the energy of the Church of God is wasted in divided efforts. Eighty thousand ministers of the gospel in the United States are doing what 20,000 could do if they were but united, and each would only have 600 members under his care—a very reasonable congregation. The other 60,000 could be sent to the heathen world, and even then there would be only one to every 2,000 of its population. The cause of this waste of energy is simply sectarianism. Each little and great body wants to be represented in every important center of population. Expense and efforts are put forth to have a church and a minister, and often it is a desperate struggle for existence for 50 or 100 poor members to support the minister and keep up a separate organization. The machinery is not worth it. It costs the same expenditure of money on the part of these people that would reach thousands of heathens by combining their energies with the church already in operation at home, and all this surplus could be spared. To a man of the world it would really look as though a wise and infinite God was not directing the movement at all, and the truth is that in a great many cases it is not God's wisdom at all, but the selfishness and folly of men.

We do not believe in attempting at this late day any formal organization, uniting all the churches, although we believe that sectarianism is unauthorized by the Scriptures. But, without attempting to revolutionize the present system of things, there are many ways in which a wise cooperation, by interdenominational methods, such as we have come to utilize in our missionary operations, would accomplish the most glorious results. Let us encourage such cooperation, and we will always find the seal and blessing of God especially set on every movement that aims at the largest unity and rises most fully above narrow and selfish sectarian lines.

John Wesley's dream is not too old to remember. The good man, in a vision of the night, found himself entering the gates of heaven, and, wanting to find some acquaintance, he asked if there were any Methodists there. They told him there were none. Any Presbyterians, but there were none. And so he went around the whole circle, but these names were all unknown. And then he looked up in astonishment and asked who was there, and they said, "We have none but Christians here; the names you speak of belong to earth, but they are unknown in heaven."

Oh, that they were lost on earth too, in the glory of Jesus' name!

The Symbols of Unity

God has given us two symbols of the unity of His Church. One is the building and the other is the Body.

The building is composed of various parts all so fitly framed together that they constitute a whole. There are foundations, arches, pillars, windows and various vessels. Some of them are very small and insignificant, and others very costly. But all are important, and the loss of a little brick or a single stone might endanger the whole structure. And so in the great house of God there are many parts. Some of them are as obscure as the concrete that lies beneath the foundation or the mortar that fills the spaces and cements the stones together or the filling in between the great masses of stone. But the very least is important, and the cement is more important even than the stones.

The humblest member has a place, and the failure of a single member will often involve the suffering and loss of a great many. The keystone of an arch is necessary to keep the arch together. The loss of a single step on the front porch may lead to accident and even to death on the part of someone entering the house. The lost shingle in a roof will often ruin the whole ceiling by leakage.

And so in the church of God you may be only a piece of flooring, you may be only a roof shingle, you may be only the front doorstep; but if you do not fulfill your place, or if you get detached from your next neighbor, you may cause the wreck of the whole building and the injury of many souls.

Still more exquisitely perfect is the figure of the human body. It consists of many members but the least of them is often the most important and receives the most abundant honor. There is an absolute necessity for their perfect harmony and adjustment in order to the health of the body. If the joint does not work in the socket the whole limb becomes diseased; and so, if you and your brother are not in harmony you hurt everybody who is within reach of you. The smallest irritation will sometimes cause the members serious inflammation. A little clot of blood will stop the action of the heart. The finest deposit upon the delicate structures of the body will prevent their free action. A scratch will often bring an abscess, and a little thorn if not removed may cause the amputation of the whole hand.

And so it is in the body of Christ. We have power to hurt one another by being hurt ourselves, and, if we would preserve the unity of the whole and the health of the whole, we must be sure that we act in perfect adjustment with those that stand next to us in every way. Not only is this true, but there is an intense sympathy between the various members of the body. If one member suffers, all suffer; if one rejoices, all rejoice. If my little finger is hurt, my heart will ache with the pain and my brain will send a throb of sympathy to the suffering member. And so in the body of Christ, the hurt of each affects the whole and God would have us share in perfect sympathy one another's needs and sorrows.

We need each other for the lightest spiritual growth. The whole body is nourished by joints and pains and blood vessels. No part can stand alone, and so none of us is independent of our brother. Let us try to receive our life through one another. Let us touch each other in whole oneness that He can minister through every part to the whole, and the beautiful figure of the apostle will be true of both the body and the building.

"In him the whole building is joined together and rises to become a holy temple in the Lord" (Ephesians 2:21). "From him the whole body, joined and held together by every supporting ligament, grows and builds itself up in love, as each part does its work" (4:16).

I can learn from the humblest child of God. The youngest convert adds something to me. Every Christian that is enriched can enrich me, and I cannot bless another without receiving as much again.

Oh, let us make the most of this blessed partnership for our own grace and His glory.

The Blessings and Benefits of Christian Unity

1. Our Spiritual Growth

It is necessary to our highest spiritual growth that "they be brought to complete unity" (John 17:23). Everything in nature and grace has a tendency to multiply. Put a little seed in the ground and it will grow with a dozen stalks and stems, and each will be stronger than if there were but a single stalk. A single coal will die out, but a hearth full of coals will brightly burn and each will kindle the other. Fellowship is essential to our spiritual blessing and "together with all the saints, [we] grasp how wide and long and high and deep is the love of Christ, and to know this love that surpasses knowledge" (Ephesians 3:18-19).

The isolated Christian is likely to be selfish and angular. We need the touch of other lives to sweeten us, to broaden us, to polish us. Even the very trials that come to us from others are the greatest blessings in our spiritual culture, sharpening and polishing us even as diamonds are necessary to polish diamonds.

2. *Impressing the World*

The unity of the Church is God's great means of impressing the world with the truth of Christianity. It is in the living fellowship of holy love that men see and feel the presence and power of God and are drawn to the Father's house. "By this all men will know that you are my disciples, if you love one another" (John 13:35); "that all of them may be one, . . . that the world may believe that you have sent me" (17:21).

Practical Suggestions

Here are some practical suggestions to promote Christian unity.

1. *Our Earnest Endeavor*

Let unity be our earnest endeavor. "Endeavoring to keep the unity of the Spirit in the bond of peace" (Ephesians 4:3, KJV).

This word *endeavor* means to strive with great earnestness, and to make it our intense desire and effort. "If it is possible, as far as it depends on you, live at peace with everyone" (Romans 12:18). If you resolve to do this under all circumstances, God will enable you. If you recognize it as being a sacred obligation as great as the Ten Commandments, you will not dare to break the law of love. If you feel that the Father and the Son might just as well be torn apart as our unity be severed with God's children, you will guard against it in every way. You will bind yourselves by the most solemn obligations which come from the cross of Christ to hold us from breaking that hidden cord that binds us to the body, just as the mother is bound to her baby.

2. *Live in Harmony*

Let us recognize the fact that God expects us to live in harmony with all the people with whom He has associated us. He wants to make us equal to every situation, and He is able to. He wants us to feel that it is a discredit and dishonor for us even to fail in living in accord with all His children. There is no one in our life that God has not somehow allowed to come and He is able to carry us successfully in every relation so to be adjusted to people, that we will be able to live with them harmoniously, sweetly, to win their respect if not their love.

Someone once asked a conductor on an express train how it was that he could put up with so many annoyances and be so agreeable under all circumstances. He said that if he could not get along on this train they would put him on the freight train. It is a good thing to remember that if we cannot get along in the delicate and difficult situations with which our Master entrusts us, He will have to put us in some easier place and withdraw some of the peace which He has given us. We can have an easy life if we want it, free from all annoyance, but we will lose much from our character and our reward. If we want to be with agreeable people all the time, God can take us to heaven where there is nothing to offend, or He can put us on some lower plane where we will have a life of freedom from these tests. But He loves us so well that He wants to discipline us and train us for the highest things and give us a richer crown. Every victory we win will bring us more in that day, and indeed much more today.

Do not ask God to excuse you from your hard place, but ask Him to fit you for it and make you more than conqueror through it.

3. Recognize the Adversary

Recognize not only God, but the adversary in many of the things that come to you, and they will not be so hard to overcome. Do not see the people irritating you, but see back of them the adversary trying to trip you. Do not give him the chance to glory over you, and you will rise above people and circumstances and see only the spiritual cause back of you. Thus you will be able to overcome many trying things.

4. Ignore Evil and Reckon It Dead

Do not try to love the evil in people or to be in unison with it, but simply ignore it and reckon it dead, as you do the evil in yourself. Feel your way to the divine in them, to the Holy Spirit in them, and love that even when you cannot love all that you see in them. Personally, when you find anything in yourself that tries you, you are glad to lay it over on Christ and refuse to recognize it any more but take Christ for it. Do the same with your brother, and it will be very strange if you cannot find enough of God in every human being to constitute a bond of unbroken fellowship, notwithstanding all their frailties and their failures.

5. *Keep Right with Those Close to You*

Keep right with the one next to you. It is always the nearest link that affects us most, and it is the one that touches you the most closely that the enemy will often use to break your unity with others. Keep in close and perfect fellowship with all who touch your life.

6. *Take the Scriptural Way*

Take the scriptural way of settling your difficulties with people. Christ has prescribed a method by which we can keep everything right with one another, and if we will do just as He has told us we will always be able to live in harmony and love. "If you are offering your gift at the altar and there remember that your brother has something against you, leave your gift there in front of the altar. First go and be reconciled to your brother; then come and offer your gift" (Matthew 5:23-24). This is a divine command just as sacred as the sixth or eighth commandment. You must get right with man before you attempt to worship God, and even at the very altar of Jehovah if you remember that there is a grievance upon your brother's heart, before you attempt to pray, go and get into full accord with him. Get the grievance out. It may not be that you have wronged him, but even if he thinks you have, go as far as you can in meeting him in the spirit of love, and then come, and the Holy Spirit will pour down upon you the fullness of His blessing.

A very small thorn penetrating your flesh will soon cause a serious inflammation. You may try all you like to suppress the inflammation, but you cannot until you pull out the thorn. If you leave the rankling stub there it will fret and fester, and by the next day there will be an angry swelling, and before a week there may be mortification and possibly amputation, and even death. Do not try to get the inflammation out, get the thorn out. Get right to the root of the thing. Begin at the trifle where all the trouble started. Recognize it. Remove it. Meet in love, and then go on in the love and blessing of God.

7. *Settle Your Troubles*

Settle your troubles with people at the throne of grace. Talk to your Father about them in love and prayer, and you will find His Holy Spirit will love to come and smooth away the rough places and make your spirit sweet. And as you pray for them, you will find the strangest warmth possess your heart and the divinest love lift you above all the stings of selfishness and pain. You cannot pray for people long without truly loving them. If you will only promise to pray every day of your life this simple prayer for any human being that you do not love, "Lord, bless her" or "Lord, bless him," with all your heart in every way as much as it is possible for them to receive, you will find before a year that they will be your dearest friend. And you will find that, as the love is borne in your heart, there will spring in their hearts such a love to you as will make them incapable of doing you any wrong.

A very dear friend of mine had a bitter alienation come up in his life with two Christian friends who had greatly injured him. He was their pastor. For months his soul was given up to perfect hate, and he did not want to love them, but one night God bade him pray for them. As he prayed, in spite of himself, his soul became flooded with such a love as he had never felt for any human being before, and he just longed to meet them and take them by the hand. There was no explanation. It was just a baptism of the Holy Spirit. But the strangest and sweetest part of it was that when he returned to his home and stood in his pulpit for the first time after a long absence, those two men had the same baptism as he had had, and they were the first to rush forward to meet him and almost took him in their arms and told him how glad they were to see him.

The same spirit that came to Jacob at Peniel and then met Esau on the way with a spirit of reconciliation and love is still able to touch our heart and prove the truth of that wonderful promise, "When a man's ways are pleasing to the LORD, he makes even his enemies live at peace with him" (Proverbs 16:7).

8. *Take a Large View of the Church*

Take a large view of the Church of God. Get beyond your immediate surroundings, your nearest friend or enemies, and learn to think of the whole kingdom of Christ as your trust to love and pray for. Regard yourself as the Bride of the Lamb and a representative of Christ for the whole world. Think of yourself as trustee of every part of the kingdom of God, and so you will get to be interested in it all. You will be lifted out of your littleness. Your soul will take on a majesty and a grandeur that others do not know, and your nobleness of purpose will prepare you for equal nobleness of service. There are most humble men and women in obscure places who are really bishops of the Church of God and can say as the great-hearted Wesley, "The world is my parish."

The truth is, if a man has a whole heart for Christ in him, he will be as big as the world in his sympathies. Christ is looking for great-hearted people. The world has plenty of intellect, but God wants something better. He wants expanded, boundless hearts in which He can dwell and from which He can bless the universe. God will give you as much as you are able to love.

Beloved, be very sure of this. The one test and condition of the highest service is the power of loving, and of loving under all circumstances with a love that loves to the end and never fails.

9. *Keep Filled with Christ*

As the secret of all, keep filled with Christ! Receive the Holy Spirit! Be filled with the Spirit and let this be evermore your prayer:

> Help me to love like Thee;
> Help me to love like Thee;
> By Thy wonderful power,
> By Thy grace every hour,
> Help me to love like Thee.

The Divine Portrait of Love

> *Love is patient, love is kind. It does not envy,*
> *it does not boast, it is not proud. It is not rude,*
> *it is not self-seeking, it is not easily angered, it*
> *keeps no record of wrongs. Love does not*
> *delight in evil but rejoices with the truth. It*
> *always protects, always trusts, always hopes,*
> *always perseveres.*
>
> *Love never fails. But where there are*
> *prophecies, they will cease; where there are*
> *tongues, they will be stilled; where there is*
> *knowledge, it will pass away. (1 Corinthians*
> *13:4-8)*

We have often looked at these verses as a picture of the ideal Christ life. Let us look at them as a living portrait of Christ Himself. There is one Man who has lived this ideal out. There is One who has crystallized this divine conception into living thoughts and words and deeds. There is One of whom it can be said that this life is possible, practicable and actual.

119

A man has succeeded in the great experiment of a heavenly life on earth, and what man has done once, man can do again. For after all, a holy life is just the reproduction of Christ in human life. We need first to see this life in Him, and then to take Him to re-enact it in us. Let's behold the glorious portrait and read the verses in the living light of His example. "Jesus is patient and kind; Jesus always protects, always trusts, always hopes, always perseveres. Jesus never fails."

This chapter contains three clusters of graces and qualities of love. There are eight negative qualities, three passive and four positive qualities. Let us look at them in detail.

Negative Qualities

1. Envy

Love does not envy. Need we say Christ does not envy? Envy is that quality of our fallen nature which looks with displeasure upon the happiness and prosperity of others and covets it for ourselves. In contrast with it, love delights in the happiness of others and wishes them well, even if we ourselves are destitute of the things they enjoy, and even if they are our friends. Jesus was incapable of envy. Almost every one around Him had more earthly comfort and wealth than He did. They had their friends and families. He was a stranger to His own country. They had their homes and possessions. He had nowhere to lay His head. They had their thrones and kingdoms, which He might have had if He wished, but He was despised and rejected of men, and yet He did not envy the lot of any man.

The reason was that He had something better in His Father's love, in His own joy and in His glorious, future destiny. He knew He had something better than all the world could give. Therefore, He was lifted above the possibility of envy. And so we will find that faith will lift us into love. If we really believe in our inheritance and realize our high place and calling, we will envy no man's lot. But we will be able to rejoice in all the happiness that God can give to any of our fellow creatures and not for a moment wish to change places with a mortal.

Beloved, do you have the faith and love that lift you above all envy and covetous desire? If you have the heart of Christ within you, you surely have.

2. Boasting

Love does not boast. Self-praise is that weak and foolish passion in human beings which loves to make a display and have the admiration of others. It loves to dress in splendid array, to make a good appearance, to be introduced in the most favorable aspect, to be spoken of highly, to be praised and exalted in the eyes of men and to cover itself with earthly honor and glory. Thus the kings of ancient times came in royal pageantry and dazzled the superficial gaze of the world with their splendid pomp. But Jesus came in lowly guise through the manger bed and the obscurity of a despised mother and a disreputable Galilean town. He never sought to attract the attention of the world by display of any kind. He appeared among men as a lowly pilgrim. He walked through Galilee and Judea as a humble stranger.

He did not even use His extraordinary miracles to build up a splendid reputation. He would not use His supernatural power at the devil's bidding to dazzle the multitudes and win the honor and homage of men. Even when He came as a King to His throne in Jerusalem, He rode upon a little colt in lowly guise. Although the sun itself put on mourning at His death and the earth shuddered in sympathetic horror, yet He Himself died in ig-nominious lowliness on the criminal's cross and was buried in a stranger's grave. He had no funeral pomp. Even the poor women that came to anoint His body were too late to pay the honors they had wished. It was not until He had left earth for heaven that the glories and honors that belonged to His royal estate were paid Him by the angels of the ascension.

His whole earthly pathway was one of lowliness and simplicity. And so if the Christ heart is in us we will be humble, too. We will not want men to think of us highly. We will wish to hide our names and faces on His breast, behind His cross and in His work. We will not bear great titles to our names. We will not have flaring advertise-ments of our work. We will not ask praise from men. We will stand with veiled face and bowed head and heavenly humility. We will be found with Him kneeling at the disciples' feet, girded with towels, and washing the feet of the saints. And even if we have the wings of the seraphim, we will use two of them to cover our faces and two of them to cover our feet, lest we or others should see ourselves or our service.

Beloved, have we the Christ love that does not boast and will not suffer others to brag about us either? Rather, do we feel a deep heart-piercing wound whenever any glory is given us that belongs only to Him?

3. Pride

Love is not proud. How true this was of Him! This expression differs from the former as pride differs from vanity. Vanity wants others to admire us, while pride thinks highly of ourselves and cares little what others think. Many persons are very proud who really look extremely humble. True humility thinks rightly of ourselves. How did Christ think of Himself? Just this:

Who, being in very nature God,
    did not consider equality with God some-
thing to be grasped,
but made himself nothing,
    taking the very nature of a servant,
    being made in human likeness.
And being found in appearance as a man,
    he humbled himself

and became obedient to death—
even death on a cross!
(Philippians 2:6-8)

Listen again to Him. "The Son can do nothing by himself" (John 5:19). "These words you hear are not my own; they belong to the Father who sent me" (14:24). His life was one of constant dependence upon God. He took the place of a helpless man and ever recognized His Father's authority and His Father's power in all He did and said.

At the same time we see in Him a beautiful simplicity. This was not self-degradation. He could think of His true place in the Father's love and His divine glory without self-exaltation. And so in truly humble hearts there is this simplicity. They can be either exalted or abased, and they are equally unconscious of self. In fact, humility is not to think meanly of yourself, but really not to think of yourself at all. And so we see in the lowliest spirits the greatest freedom even in speaking of their own work to others.

I remember hearing that eminent saint, George Müller, tell of his marvelous work of faith, and his own name occurred in nearly every sentence, but there was no self-consciousness of the man himself. So Jesus spoke constantly of Himself, but there was no consciousness or egotism in it. You feel in all He says that He is speaking just right.

Like a little child that can be the object of every eye or sit unnoticed amid its toys unconscious of itself, so true humility is so occupied with Christ and Christ's work that it is artless and lost to self altogether. And the child of God can feel that he is nothing in himself but a ransomed sinner and has nothing but what the grace of God has given, and yet he can sing with royal majesty, "I'm the child of a King."

4. Rudeness

Love is not rude. How true this was of Christ! When was He ever harsh, rude or inconsiderate of others? The Christian is the highest gentleman or lady. Christ was ever refined, courteous, gentle and heavenly in His manners. There must have been an inexpressible charm about His bearing, His look, His every act. The officers who came to arrest Him could not touch Him. They were spellbound in His presence and by His words. When His enemies arrested Him, they had to do it under cover of the night and through the treachery of a friend.

He never was entangled in His words nor found in any rude or hasty expression. He was so gentle that the little children came to Him unbidden, and poor sinners felt at home in His blessed presence.

Was there ever a touch of gallantry so exquisite as the way He treated the poor woman whom they had dragged into His presence, caught by her enemies in the act of sin and brutally exposed by their cruel charges? As they dragged her in before Him, He would not even look into her crimson face nor let her see that He heard their words. But bending down He wrote upon the ground as if He had not heard them. Then he dropped into each of their hearts a little coal of fire in the form of a hard searching question, and when they were convicted of their own conscience they all stole out of His presence. Then for the first time He rose and looked at her with beaming tenderness, only to say, "Neither do I condemn you. . . . Go now and leave your life of sin" (John 8:11).

When poor Peter had to pay his taxes and he did not have the money to pay, Jesus with thoughtful consideration noticed his embarrassment before Peter spoke of it. He sent Peter down to the sea to catch a fish with a piece of gold in its mouth, and then said, "Give it to them for my tax and yours" (Matthew 17:27). He put Himself first in the place of humiliation, and with gentle thoughtfulness relieved His embarrassed disciple from his distress.

If the heart of Christ is in us we will always be tender toward the feelings of others. We will never cut people. We will never allow ourselves the hard look, the stiff manner and chilling grasp of the hand, the tone that cuts like tempered steel, the phrases that insinuate more than they express and send gall to human hearts. But we will have that manner of "love the Father has lavished on us" (1 John 3:1).

5. *Self-seeking*

Love is not self-seeking. Was there ever anything so true of Jesus as this? Was there ever life so utterly laid down, or spirit so supremely unselfish? He gave up His high and glorious place upon the throne and forever has become one with our redeemed race, clothed in creature form although the eternal Deity. His whole earthly life was the subordination of His will, and for one who has always ruled to be subject is indeed a strange and infinite self-renunciation.

His very purpose in coming to earth was to give Himself away and every act of His earthly life was a self-renunciation, until at last upon the cross it was consummated in a sacrifice so complete that even His enemies said of Him, "He saved others, . . . but he can't save himself" (Mark 15:31).

Even the very results of His redeeming work He has allowed others than Himself to reap. His own earthly ministry ended in a little company of about 500 disciples; but to His apostles He gave on the day of Pentecost thousands of souls. He has left all the fruit to be borne by the branches of the vine, while He Himself is like the hidden root beneath the ground. He has given to us not only His precious life but Himself, His Father's love, His very glory, and when the crowning day comes He will concentrate upon His Bride the glories of the New Jerusalem, and He will shine forever reflected in us, His redeemed ones. And so, if we have in us the Christ, we also will have a life of self-renunciation.

The meaning of self-denial is not an infliction of personal torment nor penance, but it is simply the giving up of the very principle of living for ourselves. It is completely changing the direction of our being and will, so that no longer in any sense do we act with reference to how anything will affect us, but our one thought is how it will affect God or others. When we do this we are saved from self and from a thousand miseries besides.

Let me ask if nearly all your troubles have not arisen from this one fact, that you have thought of something concerning how it affected you. It was painful and irritating because it had unfavorably affected you. Yet it might have been a great blessing to somebody else and brought joy to them or, better still, to God Himself. If you had thought of this, you would have been able to rejoice in it for His sake, and say as Ignatius when the lion was about to devour him, "God has made me bread for His elect, and if it be needful that the bread must be ground in the teeth of the lion to feed His children, blessed be the name of the Lord."

Beloved, it will work an infinite revolution in your life if from this moment you will act on the simple principle of considering everything no longer as it affects you, but as it affects Christ and others. You ought to have no business any more with yourself, but live entirely to God and live only for Him. This is not only holiness, but this is heaven.

6. Angered

Love is not easily angered. In the old version it reads, "Love is not easily provoked." This might be the right way to read it if we were talking about human love, but who would dare to say Jesus was not easily provoked. In the original reading there is no "easily" and so we say, "Jesus was not provoked." Not once did He yield to the temptation to be angry. Often He might have been provoked, for He had cause to be provoked.

When He saw the wrong and injustice of men who sinned with impunity and trampled on every human right with contempt, He might have been provoked, but He was not provoked. When He saw the hypocritical Pharisees binding on men's shoulders burdens impossible to be borne and refusing to touch them with one of their fingers, He might have been provoked, but He was not. When the disciple who had walked by His side for three and a half years became His betrayer and with a treacherous kiss turned Him over to His murderers, surely He might have been provoked. But, instead, He only met him with the tenderest reproach as though He would still save him from his wicked folly and crime, and said: "Judas, are you betraying the Son of Man with a kiss?" (Luke 22:48). When Peter, His bold and boastful disciple, turned against Him in the moment of His loneliness and trial and with oaths and curses denied that he ever knew Him, Jesus was not provoked. He only thought of how He could save Peter from the remorse that was to hurl Judas into perdition. And oh, how He longed to meet his eye and give him one look of patient, forgiving, encouraging love and save him from his sin!

When they stripped Him in the judgment hall and beat Him in brutal cruelty and scorn, insulting His holy manhood in every conceivable and devilish way, not once was He provoked. So majestic was His dignified patience and sweetness, that, as He stood, bleeding and pale before them, Pilate's hard heart was touched and he was compelled to point to Him and say: "Here is the man" (John 19:5).

And so if the heart of Christ beats in our breast we will not be provoked. We will not under any circumstances feel ourselves at liberty to be vindictive, resentful, angry, violent nor overcome by passion. Rather, we will be kept like Him, in gentleness and quietness, feeling it a greater victory to be held in patience than to prostrate our enemies by a word of omnipotent power.

He could have done this in an instant, and He did it for one instant to show them His power (see John 18:6), but it was a greater victory for Him to bear it with sweetness and patience. This victory of love He fully won.

Dear friends, Christ can keep you still if you really want Him to and give Him the right, and then when the test comes, hand yourself over to Him and wholly consent with an honest purpose to be kept.

7. *Record of Wrongs*

Love does not keep a record of wrongs. This really means it makes no account of the evil, does not lay it up in store for future revenge, but gladly and quickly forgets it.

How true this was of Christ! His every business was to forgive sin and forget it, and for centuries He has been engaged in little less than blotting out the records of sin from the books of God and the tablets of His own memory, and He began to do it while He lived.

We have already spoken of His gentleness and patience toward those who wronged Him, but more beautiful than all that we have said was His dying prayer for the men who crucified Him. Even the Old Testament prophets had said: "May the LORD see this and call you to account" (2 Chronicles 24:22). But His last prayer was: "Father, forgive them, for they do not know what they are doing" (Luke 23:34). And all the years that followed, from the heavens where He ascended, He has been carrying out that loving prayer, leading one after another to receive His mercy.

The men who were saved on the day of Pentecost were the men who murdered Him. The very apostle who came nearest to His bosom for half a century, the glorious Paul, was one of His bitterest persecutors. And even yet His grace shines most conspicuously toward those who have most opposed Him and grieved Him.

The same spirit ever shines conspicuously in those in whom He dwells. A sanctified Christian cannot cherish grudges and keep grievances. We dare not lay up any account against a brother even for a single night, or we cannot claim His full forgiveness for ourselves. The Christ love in our hearts will blot out every memory and leave the tablets fresh and clean for nothing but records of love.

8. Delight in Evil

Love does not delight in evil. How easy it is for us to take pleasure in the sins of others if they have professed superior sanctity and condemned us! What a subtle satisfaction there is in thinking ourselves superior to someone else who has professed more than we, or in discovering a fault in a brother who has had some advantage of us!

The Lord Jesus took no pleasure in the sins of others, but was ever glad to recognize and forgive even His enemies. He was anxious to bury every fault and every memory of a fault in the oblivion of His love. If the heart of Christ throbs in our breasts, our great business will be to cover sin. We will not be found exposing the faults of others, but healing and concealing them.

Early in my ministry I learned a precious lesson from an old Scotch minister. One of his people once came to him with a sad complaint against a brother Christian. After listening a while to him, he said, "Have you told anybody else?" The man said, "No." "Then," said he, "go home and never speak of it while you live. If God wants to bring a scandal upon His Church, let Him do it, but do not you be the one through whom the offence cometh."

Love covers all sins, and the love of Christ in us will ever seek to cancel all the stains of that dark sad thing that only fiends delight in and only Satan loves to expose.

Brother, sister, do you ever take enough pleasure in another's fault to repeat it? As well might you carry the carrion, which is the raven's prey, and feed it to your children. As well might you be the bearer of infection from the cholera hospital to the bosom of your family. It is filthy work and you may be quite sure that you would not speak of it or listen to it if you did not find some pleasure in it. The very fact that we can ever willingly touch it proves that we have not that love that rejoices not in iniquity.

If Christ is in your heart you will detest such things as you would some foul odor, some unclean infection, and you would fly from it and drive from your presence the man or woman who would bring to you the abominable things.

Passive Qualities

1. Is Patient

Love is patient (suffereth long, KJV). One of the greatest attributes of love is to suffer. It requires more power to suffer than to do. And yet many a shallow and impulsive nature can suffer much, and for a time seem to rise above every pressure. But it is the long-suffering, the patience, that proves the heart. It is the prolonged pressure that wears out all else but heavenly love. The love that:

> Bears and forbears, and will not tire,
> Like Stephen's, an unquenched fire.

Having loved His own, He loved them unto the end. Having chosen us, it is forevermore. When He took Peter He took him for better or worse. When He took us it was with the purpose that nothing should ever separate us from His love. When He came to bear the cross for us, He set His face steadfastly to go to Jerusalem, and He did not rest until His fiery baptism was accomplished and He had suffered all the will of God.

If we have the heart of Christ in us we will suffer long. We will let patience have its perfect work. We will stand in the fire and be found at last in our lot obedient even unto death. And we will be strengthened unto all long-suffering with joyfulness.

It is a good thing when trials have to be met for us to be prepared for the worst, and for us to go out assuming that the trial will be long, and then we will be the better prepared for it.

In this sublime picture of love the first and the last word is about suffering. The picture of love begins by suffering long and ends by persevering.

It is said that woman can suffer more than man. It is because she loves more than man. Beloved, have we the suffering love, and are we willing to have the long-suffering love that for Jesus' sake will accept the cross and the thorn and give back no retaliation, but only sweetness and love?

2. Bears

Love bears everything. This has reference to the trials that come from God. How true this was of the Son of Man! "Shall I not drink the cup the Father has given me?" (John 18:11). "Not my will, but yours be done" (Luke 22:42). These were the expressions of His perfect submission to God. It was not blind submission, it was loving submission. It was the submission that believed that back of it was the Father's heart. And so the heart of Christ in us will bear all the Father's will.

There are two ways of bearing it. One is the way of stoical hardness and inevitable submission; the other is the way of willing acquiescence, trustful surrender and filial resignation. One is bowing to the stroke of the executioner, and the other is falling into the arms of the mother, of yielding to the touch of the surgeon when you know it is to save your life. Christ had taken His Father's will because He knew it was best for others, and in the end would be best for Him, bringing a crown of glory that nothing else could win. And so, "for the joy set before him, [he] endured the cross" (Hebrews 12:2).

God give to us the submission of love that

springs from trust and sings amid the tears of sorrow:

> Thy way, not mine, O Lord!
> Though seen through many a tear,
> Let not my star of faith
> Grow dim or disappear.
> Straight to my home above
> I calmly travel on,
> And sing in life or death,
> "My Lord, Thy will be done."

3. Perseveres

Love always perseveres. This has reference to the sufferings inflicted by men. How patiently Christ endured! How unremitting the trials and annoyances of His life! With His finely sensitive and perfect nature how out of harmony He must have been with everything around Him! How rude and strange this rough and sinful world must have seemed to His refined spirit. How harsh and cruel the treatment He constantly received—born in a stable, butchered on a cross, and all His life between filled up with homelessness, insult, neglect and everything uncongenial. Yet we never hear a complaint; we never find a touch of discontent. But see Him ever patient, happy, self-forgetting and only thinking how He can please and help others. He poured out His life in constant unselfishness and self-denying service.

And so if Christ lives in us we will endure like

Him. We will expect to be tried by the people we meet. We will not look for angels in our pathway. We will take it for granted that we are to be tested in our patience, forbearance, gentleness on every side. We will come out armed against the nettles and thorns with a panoply of love. We will not wonder when we are stung and pierced, but we will regard this as the very business of our life, and study how we can most sweetly meet it, and in the most Christlike way conquer it by kindness. We will make no exceptions, but will endure all things. We will count it the proof of our Captain's confidence that He lets us have the thickest of the fight. We will take joyfully the spoiling of our goods, will count it all a joy when we fall into various temptations. We will glory in tribulations, also, "Because we know that suffering produces perseverance; perseverance, character; and character, hope. And hope does not disappoint us, because God has poured out his love into our hearts by the Holy Spirit" (Romans 5:3-5).

Beloved, this is a very high plane and nothing is equal to it but the heart of Christ Himself within you. But He was equal to it once, and He is able for it still.

Positive Qualities

1. Kind

Love is kind. Kindness is that quality which aims to make people happy, and which dispenses goodness and blessing to all with whom it comes in contact. It shows itself in the genial smile, in the loving word, in the cordial pressure of the hand, in the courteous manner, in the obliging disposition, in the constant readiness to help and serve others. A truly kind person impresses you at once with his desire to communicate happiness to others. Christ so walked through the world that everybody He touched was the better for it. A child could not look at Him without getting a gleam of sunshine. A sufferer could not pass by without feeling that he had a friend. His biography was summed up in this little sentence: "He went around doing good" (Acts 10:38).

We know a few such people. Is that your character, your life? Are you uniformly kind, approachable, genial, obliging, benevolent, considerate, helpful, sympathetic, willing to serve others and always making people happier for meeting you? This is one of the things that shows itself in little touches—like the common sunshine of every day, so cheap that many despise it, but so dear and precious just because of its very homeliness. God give us the kindness of the Christ love!

2. *Truthful*

Love rejoices with the truth. Christ's love was very practical and broad; it aimed to build up the kingdom of the truth. It taught men the truth, and it saved them through it. And so, if we have Christ's love we will be witnesses for the truth.

We will rejoice in the truth. We will be found spreading the truth. We will be helpers of the truth, and the strength of our life will be invested in extending the gospel of Christ and publishing the Word of God among the nations.

The highest exercise of Christian love is the evangelization of the world.

3. Trusting

Love believes everything. This is really the secret of love; it is the flower that springs from the root of faith. It is when we fully trust God that we are able to love Him and everybody else, and it is as we trust others through Him that it is easy to love them.

The failure of love comes from the lack of confidence. When Abraham trusted God with all his heart, he could easily let go his inheritance to Lot, for he knew that Lot could not take it from him. His faith in God made him feel so secure that he was not afraid of anybody else. And so, if we have confidence in God, we will not feel that people can hurt us, and all their treatment will be unable to even irritate us.

But there is something higher even than this. We not only believe God for ourselves, but we must believe God for others. We find the Apostle Paul saying of his friends, "[I] have confidence in the Lord that you are doing and will continue to do the things we command" (2 Thessalonians 3:4). He had no confidence in them, but he had confidence in God for them. Therefore he was not tried even by their temptations and apparent failures.

If we believe in God for people, we will trust them, and even when we cannot see our faith realized we will still trust and claim the blessing and treat them as if they were real. Oh, the rest and help that it will bring to you to claim the love that believes all things! It was thus that Christ loved Peter, even when he denied Him, for His faith for Peter was looking beyond to a time when the erring apostle would be His boldest witness and with downward head would follow Him even to the cross.

Let us look at people in the light of faith as they will be in heaven when all Christ's will for them is done, and our faith will work by love and surmount even their failures and provocations.

4. *Hopeful*

Love always hopes. This was preeminently true of Christ. He was the most hopeful of all spirits. He looked not at the present, but unto the great and glorious beyond. On the Mount of Transfiguration, midway on His journey to the cross, He had caught the vision of the eternal future, and that cross was only a little speck between. But away beyond were the heights of the resurrection and ascension, the gospel age and the millennial glory, and in the light of all that it was easy to bear the trials of the present.

"For the joy set before him [he] endured the cross" (Hebrews 12:2). Yes, even despised the shame, and the glory of the future blotted out all that was dark and gloomy in the present. And His hope not only lifted Him, but it lifted all other lives into an infinite and eternal glory. He saw the future of His erring friends and even of His persecuting foes. He saw a time when those who were reviling Him would bless His name, when His love would have changed their enmity to devotion, and they would forever bless the name they were cursing then.

Let us take the hopefulness of Christ, the faith of Christ and the love of Christ and weave them together into a tablet of glory and write upon it, "Now these three remain: faith, hope and love. But the greatest of these is love" (1 Corinthians 13:13).

5. Unfailing

Love never fails. The glory of Christ's love was that it never failed.

There was a flag once in this city that had never been taken by a foe. It had been through all the battles of the war of the Union and was torn with many a shot and shell, but it had never been surrendered. Oh, there is a glory in the prestige of perpetual victory!

Beloved, you may have the Christ so within you that you will never fail. There is forever a blessing which God has for those that will take Christ for it and will let Him give it. Many a failure may come before you quite learn this secret. But it is possible, and it is for you, for He is able "to keep you from falling and to present you before his glorious presence without fault and with great joy" (Jude 24).

How will all this occur? Only as Christ Himself lives in us. This is not our love, but Christ's love. And that blessed Christ is offering Himself and His heart of love to all who will give up self forever and take Him in exchange.

The Antagonisms of Love

Love does no harm to its neighbor. Therefore love is the fulfillment of the law. (Romans 13:10)

In this chapter we will look at the shadow side of love. God often has to show us the truth more vividly in the light of its opposite.

The ancient Spartans taught their children the beauty and value of temperance by making their Helots or slaves drunk before them, that they might see the grossness and degradation of drunkenness. And so God has placed along the shores of life His beacon lights to repel us from the dangerous shoals and sunken rocks. The faith of Abel shines out more clearly in the shadow of Cain's unbelief. The character of Abraham is heightened by contrast with Lot. The choice of Jacob is made more emphatic by the profane and worldly bargain of Esau. Joseph stands out from his brothers like a star in the darkness of the night. Caleb and Joshua appear more glorious because of the unbelieving spies who accompanied them and defeated their testimony. Ruth's devotion is more beautiful in comparison with Orpah's inconsistency. And Mary's anointing receives a touch of glory from the picture of Judas' treachery. And so the Word of God has given us not only a picture of love, but also its antagonisms.

Indeed, a very large portion of our lives consists of the things that we do not do. The negative is the important element in human life and character. Just as your photograph is made from a negative, so your spiritual portrait has back of it a negative also. The Ten Commandments consist very largely of "thou shalt not." Only two of its precepts are positive; the rest are prohibitions. The portrait of love in the 13th chapter of First Corinthians is more negative than positive. Out of the 15 attributes of love, eight are things that love does not do. And so it has been playfully said, "The principal thing is to take the 'knots' out of our character, and there will be little left but love and righteousness." If we are willing to be kept from these, the Lord will give us the positive graces and qualities.

What are some of these antagonisms?

1. Self-love

Self-love is the greatest hindrance to all true love. The very essence of love is self-forgetting and living for others, and the root of depravity is the love of self. It is the antichrist of the heart. It has dethroned God from His seat and become a God unto ourselves. Therefore, the first principle of the new life is love, and the first principle of love is self-renunciation. And so the Master has said, "The man who loves his life will lose it, while the man who hates his life in this world will keep it for eternal life" (John 12:25). "For none of us lives to himself alone and none of us dies to himself alone" (Romans 14:7).

"We who are strong ought to bear with the failings of the weak and not to please ourselves. . . . For even Christ did not please himself" (15:1, 3). The enemies that kept Israel out of the land of Canaan were the Anakim, the children of Arba and Anak, and these names mean self-will and self-seeking.

And so we are kept out of our inheritance by the various forms of selfishness. You will also find that when your love has failed at any point, your gentleness has been crushed or your unity broken, it is through something that has touched you and made you think of your own interests and feel that something concerning you had suffered.

The only secret, therefore, of love is absolute self-sacrifice and complete death to the very "I" which has reigned as a rival of God and the controlling principles in your selfish heart.

2. *Selfish Love*

Self-love is the love of ourselves; selfish love is the love of somebody else for the sake of the gratification it gives us. It is the same principle working out indirectly. And so our tenderest affections may become simply a channel for the development of selfishness. We love our children and our friends because they minister to our happiness and because of the pleasure it gives us to love them, and there may be no higher principle in it all than simply the gratification of an instinct, the same in kind, although higher in degree, that the mother bird has to her brood, or the tiger to her cubs.

This comparison is very humiliating, but the logic is inexorably true. And, therefore, every human affection is to be crucified and purified in order to become heavenly love. Christ has therefore said, "Anyone who loves his father or mother more than me is not worthy of me; anyone who loves his son or daughter more than me is not worthy of me" (Matthew 10:37). "If anyone comes to me and does not hate his father and mother, his wife and children, his brothers and sisters—yes, even his own life—he cannot be my disciple. And anyone who does not carry his cross and follow me cannot be my disciple" (Luke 14:26-27).

Of course, this does not mean absolute hate. But it means such a love to Christ that everything else will be as nothing in comparison, and that love would be turned to hate if our friends separated us from Him, and we would be willing to separate from them as if they were nothing to us rather than lose His love or approval. And, therefore, we find God putting the love of His people constantly through the fire. Abraham had to give up Isaac before Isaac could be given back to him forever in holy love.

There is an awful example of this in Exodus. When Moses came down from the mount and found the people in idolatrous revelry, he called out for all who were on the Lord's side to stand up, and the sons of Levi stood up with sword in hand to vindicate the honor of Jehovah. Then Moses commanded them, "You have been set apart to the LORD today, for you were against your own sons and brothers, and he has blessed you this day" (32:29). And those true men, for God's sake, had to lift their swords and destroy their very kindred that the plague of wickedness might be stayed and the honor of God avenged. And for this reason Levi was chosen for a perpetual priesthood, and his sons were honored as the ministers of Jehovah because they loved God supremely, even over their dearest friends.

Beloved, have you consecrated yourself upon your sons and your brothers? Have you given your dearest affections to God to be held in Him, for Him and subordinate to His will in everything? I know two dear friends whose lives had been drawn together in the bonds of affection and unity and who seemed to be called to work together for the Lord as husband and wife. But I remember so well when they came to me and said, "We are too fond of each other to come together now; the temptation would be too great to live for each other rather than for God." And so God, in His gentleness and love, separated them for a time and called them to stand in single-hearted fidelity to Him. But when that had been proved and tried by the waiting, He brought them together with a love that was not earth-born, but everlasting and divine, and their lives have been one constant blessing and ministry for others.

Let no one misunderstand this. We do not mean that human affections are wrong, but they must be purified and crucified. They are like the soft shoot of the early spring which will stand no pressure. They must pass through the frost, and the next spring they are tough and hard and able to bear the fruit of the vine. The affections that are selfish are restless, absorbing, sensitive, constantly liable to be hurt and wounded by jealousy or agitated with passion. The love that is divine thinks not of its happiness nor rights, but only how it can be a blessing to others. There is a singular fact in natural history which, if true, is at least suggestive. It is said that the black widow spider loves its mate so much that in a frenzy of passion it devours it. And so there are people who love only to devour the object of their love. They want your friendship because it pleases them, and your attentions because they minister selfish delight and gratify the human.

Beloved, just apply this test for a little to your heart and your life, and you will find much need for the love that seeks not her own, and as a corollary, "is not easily angered" (1 Corinthians 13:5).

3. Hate, the Opposite of Love

It is only necessary to identify this dark and satanic passion in the light of the holy Scriptures. "But whoever hates his brother is in the darkness and walks around in the darkness; he does not know where he is going, because the darkness has blinded him" (1 John 2:11). "Anyone who does not love remains in death. Anyone who hates his brother is a murderer, and you know that no murderer has eternal life in him" (3:14-15). "Anyone who is angry with his brother will be subject to judgment. Again, anyone who says to his brother, 'Raca,' is answerable to the Sanhedrin. But anyone who says, 'You fool!' will be in danger of the fire of hell" (Matthew 5:22).

4. Anger, Rage and Malice

This trinity of evil is described in Colossians 3:8, "But now you must rid yourselves of all such things as these: anger, rage, malice." Anger is the uprising of ill-temper. Rage is the violent overflowing of ill-temper in words and acts of abuse and fury. Malice is the holding on to the ill-temper, nursing and keeping the anger in sullen resentment and bitterness. They are all contrary to love and hateful to God. And so in the lofty epistle to the Ephesians, where the apostle is speaking to the men and women who are walking in the heavenly places in Christ, he finds it necessary to warn even them against this passion. " 'In your anger do not sin': Do not let the sun go down while you are still angry" (4:26). Never let your displeasure become extreme, and never let it last beyond the close of the day, but end every day in harmony and sweetness. "Get rid of all bitterness, rage and anger, brawling and slander, along with every form of malice. Be kind and compassionate to one another, forgiving each other, just as in Christ God forgave you" (4:31-32).

5. Envy

There is something meaner, baser and more satanic even than this. It is envy, that crooked, creeping serpent that insinuates itself into the heart and looks with keen, malicious eye upon the happiness of others, and takes delight in wrecking the joys of innocence and prosperity which it cannot share. How the lightnings of God's displeasure flash over it in that wonderful book of Proverbs, which is such an unapproachable picture of the human heart! "Envy rots the bones" (14:30). "Anger is cruel and fury overwhelming, but who can stand before jealousy?" (27:4).

This is the natural condition of the human heart. And so we read in Titus 3:3: "At one time we too were foolish, disobedient, deceived and enslaved by all kinds of passions and pleasures. We lived in malice and envy, being hated and hating one another." We read again in First Peter 2:1-2: "Therefore, rid yourselves of all malice and all deceit, hypocrisy, envy, and slander of every kind. Like newborn babies, crave pure spiritual milk, so that by it you may grow up in your salvation."

6. Suspicion and Evil Surmising

Suspicion and evil surmising are two of Satan's brood of vices, classed with envy and strife in First Timothy 6:4. True love will not even harbor a thought of evil. "[Love] thinketh no evil" (1 Corinthians 13:5, KJV). In telling His Old Testament people the conditions of His blessing, God says to them in Zechariah 8:17, "Do not plot evil against your neighbor." Our love must be pure even from imagination of evil.

7. Scorn

Scorn is contrary to love. How terrible the irony with which God has said, "He mocks proud mockers but gives grace to the humble" (Proverbs 3:34).

So closely connected is this with the spirit of strife that the same inspired book says again, "Drive out the mocker, and out goes strife; quarrels and insults are ended" (22:10). We are to look down upon no human being, no matter how poor, illiterate, foolish, degraded or wicked. But we are to honor all men because they bear the image of God and to see in every human being some touch of the divine and some lingering glory from above.

8. Evil Speaking

When a physician asks you the state of your health, he is very likely to ask you to let him see your tongue. If it is coated and foul it is not hard to diagnose your disease.

Beloved, God wants to see your tongue. Love speaks no evil of his neighbor.

The book of the New Testament which corresponds to Proverbs in the Old is the epistle of James. We need no better commentary on this point than to quote a few of his sententious verses.

> If anyone considers himself religious and yet does not keep a tight rein on his tongue, he deceives himself and his religion is worthless. (1:26)

> Brothers, do not slander one another. Anyone who speaks against his brother or judges him speaks against the law and judges it. When you judge the law, you are not keeping it, but sitting in judgment on it. There is only one Lawgiver and Judge, the one who is able to save and destroy. But you—who are you to judge your neighbor? (4:11-12)

This truth is not confined to people who are wholly sinful alone. The worst of it is that it is the fault of those who love and worship God also. And so we read:

> With the tongue we praise our Lord and Father, and with it we curse men. . . . Out of the same mouth come praise and cursing. My brothers, this should not be. . . .

Who is wise and understanding among you? Let him show it by his good life, by deeds done in the humility that comes from wisdom. But if you harbor bitter envy and selfish ambition in your hearts, do not boast about it or deny the truth. Such "wisdom" does not come down from heaven but is earthly, unspiritual, of the devil. For where you have envy and selfish ambition, there you find disorder and every evil practice. (3:9-16)

9. Evil Hearing

Evil hearing is as much forbidden by the law of love as evil speaking. The man who will abide in God's tabernacle and dwell in His holy will is the man who "does his neighbor no wrong" (Psalm 15:3). The man who will "dwell on the heights" and "will see the king in his beauty and view a land that stretches afar" (Isaiah 33:16-17), is the man "who stops his ears against plots of murder and shuts his eyes against contemplating evil" (33:15). If you are walking in the law of love you will drive from your presence the man or woman who carried to you the putrid carrion of slander and calumny.

10. Unforgiveness

Unforgiveness is contrary to the law of love. In Matthew 28:21, our Savior tells His disciples that they are to forgive until 70 times 7. And in the parable of the unmerciful servant, He teaches us that unforgiveness is an unpardonable sin and as fatal as unbelief to the soul. In Hebrews 12:15, we learn that a single root of bitterness may spring up and so trouble us that many will be defiled. And in Matthew 5:23, He commands us to immediately settle every personal grievance with an offended or an offending brother, and not to go to the altar of God with even the cloud of a mutual trouble or strife.

Once more in Matthew 28:15-17, He gives us a remedy for every misunderstanding and wrong, and if we would but walk accordingly we should be able to be in peace with all men. There may be persons with whom we cannot live in peace and whose churlish spirit will not receive our love, but this is such a remote possibility that the apostle says, "If it is possible, as far as it depends on you, live at peace with everyone" (Romans 12:18).

11. *The Spirit of Judging*

The spirit of judging is forbidden by the law of love. "Do not judge, or you too will be judged. For in the same way you judge others, you will be judged, and with the measure you use, it will be measured to you" (Matthew 7:1-2). And then with sarcasm it is added, "Why do you look at the speck of sawdust in your brother's eye and pay no attention to the plank in your own eye? How can you say to your brother, 'Let me take the speck out of your eye,' when all the time there is a plank in your own eye?" (7:3-4). The Greek word for beam is rafter. It means a great log of timber. The inference is that whenever you see a little sawdust or speck in your brother's eye, it is a sure sign that you have got a great big rafter in your own eye.

There is intense force and fire in the words of the apostle in Romans 14:4: "Who are you to judge someone else's servant? To his own master he stands or falls." And then with indignant recoil he adds, "And he will stand, for the Lord is able to make him stand." The surest way to get God to vindicate a man is for you to sit in judgment upon him.

12. *Criticism and Prejudice*

Heavenly love is contrary to criticism and prejudice. Prejudice means prejudging, judging beforehand, judging from caprice or dislike, rather than from a thorough knowledge of the facts. And so it is very clearly forbidden: "Therefore judge nothing before the appointed time; wait till the Lord comes. He will bring to light what is hidden in darkness and will expose the motives of men's hearts. At that time each will receive his praise from God" (1 Corinthians 4:5). This is a very beautiful passage. There is a day coming when God will show everything in His true light, and with a loving purpose will show the good, and only the good. Someday we will understand the things that now we judge so hastily and then we will wish we could live our lives over again.

Oh, that we might be like Him who never

judges hastily, who looks at both sides, and aims only to see the good and not the evil, and loves to hide a multitude of sins. But the keen critic's eye is always looking for the flaw in the marble or the fly in the ointment. And he generally gets such a rafter in his eye that he has no trouble in seeing it projected on the retina of his vision from the piece of timber in his own eye.

Love delights to see the good and to praise where it can. How beautiful the spirit of the New Testament epistles! They always begin with commendation. Even in the Savior's letters to the seven churches of Asia, He always speaks of the kind things first.

13. Giving Offense

Giving offense is forbidden by this law. "Things that cause people to sin are bound to come," says the Master, "but woe to that person through whom they come! It would be better for him to be thrown into the sea with a millstone tied around his neck than for him to cause one of these little ones to sin" (Luke 17:1-2). "Do not cause anyone to stumble, whether Jews, Greeks, or the church of God" (1 Corinthians 10:32). This is the Spirit of Christ.

The word *offense* means cause of stumbling. We are not to be in slavish bondage to the foolish whims of others, but we are to avoid every reasonable cause of harm to their spiritual life. And if in anything our acts weaken their faith or consecration, we are responsible up to the measure of our influence.

A poor blind man was once asked why he carried a lamp at night, when he could not see its rays. He said, "I carry it to keep the people from stumbling over me." So let us walk that no man will receive anything from us but blessing, and the testimony of every human being, when we get to the Father's house, will be, "You were always a blessing and nothing but a blessing to me." Is it not a holy ambition worthy of every sacrifice?

14. Taking Offense

Taking offense is as bad as giving offense. Undue sensitiveness is real selfishness. There is a Greek word used once by the apostle which has a very singular meaning. The verse reads thus: "I want you to be wise about what is good, and innocent about what is evil" (Romans 16:19). The Greek word used here means "without horns." Some people are all horns. They get caught in the brush every time they go through the thicket. Or, they are like certain fabrics which catch all the burrs on the roadside. If there is anything to irritate or annoy, they are sure to catch it. Christ has said to such people, "These things have I spoken unto you, that ye should not be offended" (John 16:1, KJV). And there is a great promise for such souls in Psalm 119:165: "Great peace have they who love your law, and nothing can make them stumble."

If you will but love God's law and have His great peace, nothing will hurt you. And when you do get offended it is either because your heart is not single to God in obedience and entire consecration, or else you have lost His peace and joy.

Isaac Watts wrote two lines once that should be written on all our phylacteries:

> I'll not willingly offend
> Nor easily be offended.

15. *Rudeness*

Harshness of manner is contrary to love. "[Love] is not rude, it is not self-seeking, it is not easily angered, it keeps no record of wrongs" (1 Corinthians 13:5). A truly sanctified soul will always be considerate of the feelings of others and avoid the manners of the world which so deeply wound, by the studied tone, or gesture, or look of cold indifference, contempt or scorn.

16. *Falsehood and Deceit*

Falsehood and deceit are forbidden by the law of love. The Apostle Paul gives a very beautiful reason for truthfulness and frankness: "Therefore each of you must put off falsehood and speak truthfully to his neighbor, for we are all members of one body" (Ephesians 4:25). It is the body of Christ that calls for our sincerity and true-heartedness, for when we sin against our brother we sin against ourselves.

17. *Pride and Vainglory*

Pride and vainglory are contrary to love. "Do

not think of yourself more highly than you ought, but rather think of yourself with sober judgment, in accordance with the measure of faith God has given you" (Romans 12:3). And then the reason for this is the same already given for truthfulness—our unity in Christ. "Just as each of us has one body with many members, and these members do not all have the same function, so in Christ we who are many form one body, and each member belongs to all the others" (12:4-5).

The law of love will lead us to recognize our equality and to recognize every personal gift and grace as simply a bestowment of divine mercy, and to say, "What do we have that we have not received? Who makes us different?"

18. Favoritism

Favoritism of persons is forbidden by the law of love. "My brothers, as believers in our glorious Lord Jesus Christ, don't show favoritism" (James 2:1). The love of Christ in us will recognize everyone in his or her place, and relative to Christ and entitled to our consideration. The mere circumstance of wealth, culture or any earthly superiority will not justify us in giving undue prominence to one above another. But the wisdom from above will be without partiality and without hypocrisy.

19. Lawsuits

Lawsuits with God's children are forbidden by the law of love.

> If any of you has a dispute with another,
> dare he take it before the ungodly for judg-
> ment instead of before the saints? . . . But
> instead, one brother goes to law against
> another—and this in front of unbelievers!
>
> The very fact that you have lawsuits
> among you means you have been complete-
> ly defeated already. Why not rather be
> wronged? Why not rather be cheated?
> (1 Corinthians 6:1, 6-7)

The teaching of this passage is unmistakable. It
does not forbid a Christian defending himself if
attacked unjustly in the courts, but it does forbid
our going to law one with another before the
world. And it teaches us that there should be a
provision for Christian arbitration in all matters
affecting God's people.

20. Severeness

Severity to the erring is forbidden by divine
love in Second Corinthians 2:6-8. The apostle
speaks of a case of one who had been severely disciplined by his church for his sin and warns them
against the danger of undue severity and
prolonged exclusion from the fellowship of
Christians.

> The punishment inflicted on him by the
> majority is sufficient for him. Now instead,
> you ought to forgive and comfort him, so
> that he will not be overwhelmed by exces-

sive sorrow. I urge you, therefore, to reaffirm your love for him.

No matter how fallen and unworthy a man is, our love must be ready to help and save and guard him against anything that could cause him to sink or stumble in the way.

21. Discouragement

Love will show itself especially in avoiding everything that would discourage the weak. "Accept him whose faith is weak, without passing judgment on disputable matters" (Romans 14:1). There are many Christians who cannot stand what others can. And true love will not be impatient with them and intolerant because of their foolishness; but will treat them as they should be and hear and help them. Many of us have to bear with a great many peculiar Christians. The church is full of spiritual cripples, cranks and imbeciles. Love will always bear with them with tender consideration, not making sport of their peculiarity, but finding out what is good and seeking to help and cherish them, and yet with a wholesome good sense that will in no way encourage their foibles and their follies.

22. Sectarianism

Sectarianism is forbidden by Christian love. "One of you says, 'I follow Paul'; another, 'I follow Apollos'; another, 'I follow Cephas'; still another, 'I follow Christ' " (1 Corinthians 1:12).

"What, after all, is Apollos? And what is Paul? Only servants, through whom you came to believe—as the Lord has assigned to each his task" (3:5).

23. *Controversy*

Controversy is forbidden by this law:

> But avoid foolish controversies and genealogies and arguments and quarrels about the law, because these are un-profitable and useless. (Titus 3:9)

> And the Lord's servant must not quarrel; instead, he must be kind to everyone, able to teach, not resentful. Those who oppose him he must gently instruct, in the hope that God will grant them repentance lead-ing them to a knowledge of the truth.
> (2 Timothy 2:24-25)

24. *Fear*

Fear is opposed to love. "There is no fear in love. But perfect love drives out fear, because fear has to do with punishment. The one who fears is not made perfect in love" (1 John 4:18).

25. *Disobedience*

Disobedience is inconsistent with divine love. "He who does not love me will not obey my teaching" (John 14:24).

These are some of the antagonisms of love in

its twofold aspect to God and to one another. Many of them are but little things, but these are the things that mar the picture and defile the spotless purity of Christian character. Satan has no objections to your sanctification; he is quite willing that you should put on the white robe and the marriage robe. All he wants is to put a little stain upon it, a single spot, for he knows that this will defile and destroy the whole. The bride's fair garment does not need to be rent and torn, it is enough that a single speck show upon its whiteness and it is useless. The moth does not eat the whole robe, but only perforates it with tiny holes, and the costly fur and the valuable fabric is ruined forever.

Dear friends, what Christ wants is the love that never fails, and He is able to give it. Let us only see the places where the danger comes and be guarded against them and choose to stand. He will give us the grace to stand and put in us His own love and bind us to His throne with love's unbroken chain.

He does not ask us to make the love and produce the grace. He only asks us to avoid the snares and the hindrances, and to say "No" to the temptations of the adversary. If we will do this, He will do the rest. And that glorious picture will be fulfilled in which love is represented as a perfect girdle that passes all around our person and binds all the other garments together in the beauty of holiness and the adorning of the heavenly bride.

Phases and Features of Love

We have looked at the reverse side of the shield; now let us look at its face, all golden and glorious in the light of the Holy Spirit and the holy Scriptures. We have looked at love as one bright, divine and living face personified in Jesus Christ. Let us look at it now in its particular features and minute details as the New Testament portrays them in many an inspired picture.

1. Love to Christ

Let us look at our love to Christ as it shines in the life and testimony of the warmest heart that ever throbbed with the love of Jesus.

> If we are out of our mind, it is for the sake of God; . . . For Christ's love compels us, because we are convinced that one died for all, and therefore all died. And he died for all, that those who live should no longer live for themselves but for him who died for

them and was raised again. (2 Corinthians
5:13-15)

Here we behold the love of Christ as not only a
heavenly passion, but an enthusiasm so intense
that men may almost call it madness. "We are
sober enough," the apostle says, "when we look at
you, but when we look at Jesus, we are beside
ourselves." And like a great torrent whose waters
cannot be held back, our love sweeps over all
banks and barriers and constrains us to live, not
unto ourselves, but unto Him who died for us
and rose again.

This was the glory of Paul's character and this
will make any life sublime: the passion fire of
love, following the passion sign of the cross.

2. *The Church of God*

The Church of God is a family circle related in
Christ and beloved for His sake. Love to the
brethren, therefore, is one of the first instincts of
the new life and one of the tests of our growth
and spiritual healthfulness. We have many pictures of it in the New Testament. Paul writes to
the Thessalonians, "Now about brotherly love we
do not need to write to you, for you yourselves
have been taught by God to love each other. And
in fact, you do love all the brothers throughout
Macedonia. Yet we urge you, brothers, to do so
more and more" (1 Thessalonians 4:9-10).

Romans 12 is a sort of companion picture of
First Corinthians 13. There the apostle unfolds

first the great doctrine of our unity in Christ as members one of another, and then He applies it to our practical Christian relations. "Be devoted to one another in brotherly love. Honor one another above yourselves" (Romans 12:10). This is more than cold, conventional charity or ecclesiastical courtesy. This is a great deal more than the ceremonious fellowships of our church life. It is the warm grasp of the hand, the radiant smile, the loving sympathy, the tender home bond which binds the household together as one family in Him. It is a kind and affectionate love. It is the constant habit of thinking of your brother before yourself, and gladly honoring and recognizing him in his work even more than yourself.

The same picture is repeated in Ephesians 4:1-4:

As a prisoner for the Lord, then, I urge you to live a life worthy of the calling you have received. Be completely humble and gentle; be patient, bearing with one another in love. Make every effort to keep the unity of the Spirit through the bond of peace. There is one body and one Spirit—just as you were called to one hope when you were called.

This is our right attitude to all the children of God, not only in our own little sect and circle of acquaintances, but in the whole family of Christ because they belong to Christ.

3. *A Broader Love*

There is a broader love than the love of the heavenly household. Therefore we find the Apostle Peter in his portrait of a perfect Christian life bidding us to "add to your faith goodness; and to goodness, knowledge; and to knowledge, self-control; and to self-control, perseverance; and to perseverance, godliness" (2 Peter 1:5-6), and to all these the two crowning qualities of holy character "and to brotherly kindness charity" (1:7, KJV).

Brotherly kindness is our love to our brethren in Christ. Charity is our larger love to the whole world. Both of these are necessary to a perfect character. Without these, even godliness would give our spirit only one dimension, pointing upward to the sky like some great, branchless tree. God wants us rounded, developed and filled up with all the human sights that come to us through contact with men and are deepened and developed by our intercourse with our fellows.

Hence, men that have the largest contact with men are usually the largest men. A man who spends all his life in a study, a school or a prayer-meeting will be an angular, narrow ecclesiastic or a devotee as stiff as the starch in his shirt collar. The man who touches men on every side will be a rounded, symmetrical man. Hence, business men are more liberal, more mellow, and as a rule, more practical than ministers.

God wants to give us as many fillings as we will

take; therefore He does not at once take us to heaven when we are saved, but He puts us into the school of life. Amid the varieties of people with whom we come in contact, He is shaping us, polishing us and preparing us for the highest manhood and the broadest usefulness.

Now love is our equipment for all these situations. We are to meet all our brethren with brotherly kindness, and we are to meet all the people of the world with charity—a charity that never fails, but that adjusts us to every relationship and situation with a heavenly sweetness and fitness that will commend Christ in everything we do.

4. *In the Family*

Love comes into the innermost circles of human life—love in the family—and sanctifies, sweetens and elevates every human affection. Therefore in the epistles to the early Christians, husbands are to love their wives just as Christ loved the Church (Ephesians 5:25). Wives are to respond with subjection even as unto Christ, and to love not only the good and gentle, but also the unkind and froward. Parents are to bring up their children, not in the impulses of selfish affection, but in the "training and instruction of the Lord" (6:4). Children are to love and honor their parents as they do the Lord, and even servants are to forget their earthly relationships and do their work as unto Christ.

And so heavenly love hallows the home and

shines in holy luster within the sanctuary of the heart and hearth.

5. *Love Our Enemies*

And if we go to the opposite extreme from love to hate, from the home circle to the ranks of hostile foes, love still goes with us and teaches us to "Love your enemies, do good to those who hate you, bless those who curse you, pray for those who mistreat you" (Luke 6:27-28). "If your enemy is hungry, feed him; if he is thirsty, give him something to drink. In doing this, you will heap burning coals on his head" (Romans 12:20).

6. *Patience*

The highest form of love is patience, longsuffering and love toward those that only cause us pain. And so the very text of meekness for the inheritance of the saints in light is given us in Colossians 1:11-12: "being strengthened with all power according to his glorious might so that you may have great endurance and patience, and joyfully giving thanks to the Father, who has qualified you to share in the inheritance of the saints in the kingdom of light."

This is not only patience and longsuffering, but longsuffering with joyfulness. This is a love that not only endures, but surmounts the pressure and soars amid the cloudless sunshine of heaven triumphant, even above hate and pain because of the joy unspeakable that cancels every sorrow and disarms every dart.

7. *Love's Covering*

Let us look at the complete picture of love's en-
robing.

> Therefore, as God's chosen people, holy
> and dearly loved, clothe yourselves with
> compassion, kindness, humility, gentleness
> and patience. Bear with each other and for-
> give whatever grievances you may have
> against one another. Forgive as the Lord
> forgave you. And over all these virtues put
> on love, which binds them all together in
> perfect unity. (3:12-14)

Here is the entire dress of the sanctified Christian. Beginning inside with our very life, we are
to put on compassion, kindness, humility. Then
we are to wear all the outer garments of gentleness, patience, forbearance. And when the robes
are all complete we are to put around us, as the
belt that will hold them all together, that love
which is a perfect belt passing all around and
leaving no place open or exposed, but covering in
every part and compacting all our dress so that we
are prepared for every situation and victor under
every circumstance.

8. *Love in Christian Fellowship*

Let us look for a moment at love as it manifests
itself in Christian fellowship. It binds the hearts
of saints together in blessed oneness. Therefore

the apostle says, "If you have any encouragement from being united with Christ, if any comfort from his love, if any fellowship with the Spirit, if any tenderness and compassion, then make my joy complete by being like-minded, having the same love, being one in spirit and purpose" (Philippians 2:1-2). How beautiful is his own picture of his fellowship with his friends in Philippi! "I have you in my heart; for whether I am in chains or defending and confirming the gospel, all of you share in God's grace with me. God can testify how I long for all of you with the affection of Christ Jesus" (1:7-8).

Again, let us look at the tenderness of his love as he expresses it in First Thessalonians 2:8, "We love you so much that we were delighted to share with you not only the gospel of God but our lives as well, because you had become so dear to us." This is no mere human friendship. This is the love that touches God before it touches any man or woman, and it only touches them in God and is bound to them by His divine and perfect love. But it is very real, blessed and unspeakably helpful, comforting, strengthening, inspiring the heart in the service of God and giving evermore a heavenly foretaste of the fellowship above.

9. Partnership in Service

We have some lovely pictures of love as it relates to partnership in service. How suggestive are the words of Paul to the Philippians. "I ask you, loyal yokefellow, help these women who have contended at my side in the cause of the gospel, along with Clement and the rest of my fellow workers, whose names are in the book of life" (4:3).

How charming the picture of Aquila and Priscilla, who Paul calls, "my fellow workers in Christ Jesus. They risked their lives for me. Not only I but all the churches of the Gentiles are grateful to them" (Romans 16:3-4). How his directions about Phoebe speak to us in this selfish age: "Receive her in the Lord in a way worthy of the saints and . . . give her any help she may need from you, for she has been a great help to many people, including me" (16:2). How beautiful the picture of Timothy. "I have no one else like him, who takes a genuine interest in your welfare. For everyone looks out for his own interests, not those of Jesus Christ. But you know that Timothy has proved himself, because as a son with his father he has served with me in the work of the gospel" (Philippians 2:20-22). How beautiful the story of Epaphroditus whose love sought out the lonely apostle in Rome. He risked his own life that he might minister to Paul (2:26-27, 30).

10. Sympathy

Sympathy is one of the forms that love takes. In the body of Christ, one member suffers with another and feels the common pain. And so the apostle tells us to "Carry each other's burdens, and in this way you will fulfill the law of Christ"

(Galatians 6:2). He says of himself, "Who is weak, and I do not feel weak? Who is led into sin, and I do not inwardly burn?" (2 Corinthians 11:29). He counts it his glory to "fill up in my flesh what is still lacking in regard to Christ's afflictions, for the sake of his body, which is the church" (Colossians 1:24).

To share with the Master and His disciples their sufferings and pains in proportion to our love, we will suffer for those we love; and in the Holy Spirit we will often have their every need laid upon us both in soul and body that we may help them. Love gladly welcomes such burdens and glories in such pains.

11. Liberality and Benevolence

Liberality and benevolence will always keep pace with love. What charming pictures we have of the Apostolic Church in this regard! Paul came saying of them: "For I testify that they gave as much as they were able, and even beyond their ability" (2 Corinthians 8:3). First they gave themselves to the Lord, and then their means. "But," he adds, speaking to us, "just as you excel in everything—in faith, in speech, in knowledge, in complete earnestness and in your love for us—see that you also excel in this grace of giving. . . . For you know the grace of our Lord Jesus Christ, that though he was rich, yet for your sakes he became poor, so that you through his poverty might become rich" (2 Corinthians 8:7, 9).

12. *The Spirit and Ministry of Prayer*

Our love will show itself in the spirit and ministry of prayer. How very beautiful the testimony we receive of Paul in his prayers for his friends in Christ. "I thank my God every time I remember you. In all my prayers for all of you, I always pray with joy because of your partnership in the gospel from the first day until now" (Philippians 1:3-5).

Again, he says, "I want you to know how much I am struggling for you and for those at Laodicea, and for all who have not met me personally. My purpose is that they may be encouraged in heart and united in love, so that they may have the full riches of complete understanding, in order that they may know the mystery of God, namely, Christ" (Colossians 2:1-2). In another chapter he speaks of Epaphras, "who is one of you and a servant of Christ Jesus, . . . He is always wrestling in prayer for you, that you may stand firm in all the will of God, mature and fully assured" (4:12).

To the Ephesians he writes, "And pray in the Spirit on all occasions with all kinds of prayers and requests. With this in mind, be alert and always keep on praying for all the saints. Pray also for me, that whenever I open my mouth, words may be given me so that I will fearlessly make known the mystery of the gospel" (Ephesians 6:18-19).

There is no mightier help that we can give a Christian friend than prayer. There is no tenderer bond of remembrance and love than prayer. There is no meeting place more sacred, and no communion more real than that we find beneath the mercy seat.

Are we true to this ministry of love? Do we pray for one another as faithfully as the apostle did? Is our prayer list as large and wide as our list of friends? Have we that Christlike love that touches and helps those who, perhaps, have none to help them but us? May God give to us a more unselfish, indiscriminating, worldwide and mighty ministry of prayer!

13. *Courtesy and Consideration*

Christian courtesy and consideration to others will always be found as two of the many manifestations of Christian love. The Apostle Peter drops two little words that may be among the minutiae of Christian love, but they are fraught with much significance for the happiness or pain of others. "Be compassionate and humble" (1 Peter 3:8).

And the Apostle Paul has left us a beautiful commentary of these words in his letter to Philemon. The occasion of this little epistle of courtesy was the conversion of Onesimus, a former slave of Philemon. While in Rome, where he had fled from his master, he became acquainted with Paul. Paul found him a most profitable helper and would gladly have kept him, but was far too honorable and polite to do so without Philemon's consent, so he wrote this beautiful letter and sent it back to Colosse, commending the restored slave to the master's forgiveness and love, and asking for his sake that Philemon would receive him in the spirit of love. The whole letter is full of exquisite touches of tact and sanctified politeness.

He reminds him very gently of the right he might have claimed to enjoin him to do this thing, and he sweetly adds: "I appeal to you on the basis of love. I then, as Paul—an old man and now also a prisoner of Christ Jesus" (Philemon 9). He then hints how gladly he would have kept Onesimus, but gives Philemon the chance to bestow kindness on him of his own free will.

He then ventures to ask him to receive Onesimus not as a slave, but with brotherly love, and he says that if the servant had defrauded him of anything, he, Paul, would gladly make it up. Like a wise master of hearts he does not plead too strongly, but assumes with tactful confidence that his friend will do much more than he asks. Then, with the very highest tact, he gently hints that he himself is coming very soon to visit Philemon and leaves an impression that would make it exceedingly difficult for his friend to deny his request and yet meet him in his own home without embarrassment. It is indeed a masterful letter and a pattern of the very highest Christian tact.

The more truly Christ dwells in us, the more refined will every sensibility be, and the more impossible for us to hurt another's feelings if we can avoid it. At the same time, there is, of course, a limit to even kindness. There are people who compel us to be guarded for our own self-respect and for their good. And so the New Testament has taught us how to deal with idle, imposing and unworthy persons, such as are ever found like waifs stranded on the shore of every Christian movement. We are not compelled to pay a premium to indolence and dependence.

The apostle tells us in Second Thessalonians 3:11 and 14, to withdraw ourselves from every brother who walks disorderly, who does not work, who is a busybody. Yet we are not to count such an one as an enemy, but to admonish him as a brother. And again, in the second epistle of John, we read of persons who are not worthy of our fullest confidence, and to whom we cannot bid Godspeed or we shall be partakers of their evil deeds. But this must all be done with love and tenderness.

There is a most beautiful passage in the epistle to the Colossians (3:16) which sets our rebukes to music and bids us to admonish one another, if we have to do it, in psalms and hymns and spiritual songs.

There is no duty so difficult as that of speaking plainly to the erring, and no place where Christian love can so display its finer qualities and its freedom from the coarseness, harshness and rudeness of the natural heart. God give us the tenderness, compassion and courtesy of Christ!

14. *Speaking the Truth in Love*

We have some fine examples of an affectionate ministry in the New Testament. It is possible to teach and preach the gospel with all truthfulness, and yet without love. Our great power is in speaking the truth in love. The ministry that will accomplish most is that which beseeches man "on Christ's behalf: [to] Be reconciled to God" (2 Corinthians 5:20). How very beautiful is this spirit in Paul! Could anything be tenderer than this: "we were gentle among you, like a mother caring for her little children. . . . For you know that we dealt with each of you as a father deals with his own children" (1 Thessalonians 2:7, 11).

15. Ministry for the Lost

It is especially in our ministry for the lost that the love of Christ must constrain us if we would have power. We need not preach to sinners unless we do it tenderly. As the Apostle Paul spoke of the enemies of the cross of Christ and their awful end he did it "even with tears" (Philippians 3:18). And in writing to the Roman Christians about his own countrymen, the Jews, he rises to a height of passionate tenderness which has never been approached except by the Spirit of the Master in Moses and Jeremiah in the days of old. How many of us are able to understand and feel the meaning of these words: "Brothers, my heart's desire and prayer to God for the Israelites is that they may be saved" (Romans 10:1). And of the still more unapproachable words:

> I speak the truth in Christ—I am not lying, my conscience confirms it in the Holy Spirit—I have great sorrow and unceasing anguish in my heart. For I could wish that I myself were cursed and cut off

from Christ for the sake of my brothers,
those of my own race, the people of Israel.
(9:1-4)

Such a man must draw souls to Christ, for he
binds around them his very heart strings and
draws them by the cords of love.

Such then are some of the phases of Christian
love. It is a great thing to see them and see our
failures in them and the victories of grace and virtue which we may take from Him and transfer to
our own life and character.

A few years ago [the 1890s] there were many
people interested in a simple and popular form of
art, known as transferring pictures and commonly
called decalcomania. These pictures were not
drawn by the artist, but were obtained ready
made, and by a delicate touch had simply to be
cut out of the tissue paper and transferred to the
article to be ornamented. Being pressed down
with a hot iron, they adhered to the surface and
really became a part of the piece of furniture or
beautiful page to be adorned. So in our spiritual
life, God gives us His transfer pictures in His
great treasury of grace, and we have just to set
them in our life where we are inadequate and un-
equal to the pressure, and the Holy Spirit will
burn them in.

There are three steps we must take in realizing
this experience of putting on the Lord Jesus
Christ and His grace. First, we must choose the
love of Christ, and let Him see that we mean it.

Second, we must take it by simple faith from Him, as something not in us, but in Him for us. Third, when the real situation comes in life, we must let Him work it into us. We must not flinch under the temptation or seeming failure, but stand true to the position we have taken, and He will graciously and wholly accomplish His work in us and bring us into the realization of all that we have claimed.

And so you shall "add to your faith goodness; and to goodness, knowledge; and to knowledge, self-control; and to self-control, perseverance; and to perseverance, godliness; and to godliness, brotherly kindness; and to brotherly kindness, love" (2 Peter 1:5-7). And thus our Christian character will grow into symmetrical fullness, and we will reach, at length, the fullness of the stature of Christ Jesus and that life divine whose essence is love.

And so "May the Lord make your love increase and overflow for each other and for everyone else. . . . May he strengthen your hearts so that you will be blameless and holy in the presence of our God and Father when our Lord Jesus comes with all his holy ones" (1 Thessalonians 3:12-13).